D1072858

NEWMAN

Avery Cardinal Dulles SJ

continuum

Continuum

The Tower Building, 11 York Road, London, SE1 7NX
Suite 704, 80 Maiden Lane, New York, NY 10038, USA

www.continuumbooks.com

© Avery Cardinal Dulles SJ 2002

All rights reserved. No part of this publication may be reproduced or transmitted
in any form or by any means, electronic or mechanical, including photocopying,
recording or any information storage or retrieval system, without prior permission
from the publishers.

First published 2002
Second edition published 2005
This edition published 2009

British Library Cataloguing-in-Publication Data
A catalogue record for this book is available from The British Library

ISBN 978-08264-3564-4

Typeset by BookEns Ltd, Royston, Herts.
Printed and bound by MPG Books Ltd., Bodmin, Cornwall

Contents

Foreword

It was an excellent idea to ask the distinguished theologian Cardinal Avery Dulles, who would not claim to be a Newman specialist, to write an introductory book about Newman. As Dulles notes, there is a lack – strangely enough given the enormous amount that has been written on Newman – of 'a volume that strives, as I do here, to survey Newman's teaching about the classical theological questions in a comprehensive and systematic way'.

Writing as a contemporary theologian, and like Newman himself a convert to Catholicism and elevated to the College of Cardinals in recognition of his theological achievement, Dulles provides valuable perspectives on Newman for both specialist and general reader. On the one hand, he provides a very useful, succinct, and readable account of Newman's theology; and on the other hand, he offers a critique of it from the standpoint of a Catholic theologian writing in the wake of the Second Vatican Council, which Newman anticipated in a number of ways in his own writings.

Dulles has authoritative and illuminating chapters on 'Newman's pilgrimage of faith', 'Redemption, justification, and sanctification', 'Faith and reason', 'The proof of Christianity', 'Revelation, doctrine, and development', 'The Church as organ of revelation', 'The roles of theologian and the laity', 'The Church and the Churches', and 'The University'. On the development of doctrine, he writes: 'This single work, far more than any other, established the idea of doctrinal development as a principle of Catholic theology. Although much has been written on the subject since Newman's time, it would be difficult to name any rival treatise that measures up to his in depth and thoroughness.' Dulles also singles out Newman's anticipation of the thought of Karl Rahner 'to the effect that every dogmatic proclamation is not only an end but also a beginning. The decision of any one question opens up new questions for the theological schools.' In the area of ecclesiology, Dulles praises Newman's 'treatment of the three offices' of the Church as 'highly original', differing 'markedly from the continental tradition of Catholic theology', which ascribed 'all three offices in their fullness to the pope and bishops' alone. And he commends Newman for emphasising the inevitable 'tension' between the offices rather than merely their 'harmony', as Vatican II does.

In a final chapter of assessment, 'Newman in Retrospect', Dulles sums up Newman's theological achievement, concluding that 'His most enduring contributions were in the realm of what we today call fundamental theology', with regard particularly to the relation between faith and reason, but also doctrinal development. This would seem to understate Newman's contribution to ecclesiology, which emerged as practically a new branch of theology in the nineteenth century. Newman certainly anticipated Vatican II's understanding of faith and revelation, but his anticipation of the Council's understanding of the Church – and Vatican II was the first General Council to be almost exclusively concerned with the nature of the Church and its internal and external aspects – was surely at least as remarkable. The French *ressourcement*, or retrieval of the scriptural and patristic sources, without which the Council's Constitution on the Church could hardly have been formulated, had already been pioneered by Newman and his Tractarian colleagues in the Oxford of the 1830s a hundred years before. I would therefore want to modify Dulles's assertion that 'the Council went considerably beyond Newman in ... its sacramental ecclesiology'. The Anglican Newman had surely already grasped the essentials of the scriptural and patristic teaching on the fundamental nature of the Church that the Council put forward in the first two chapters of *Lumen Gentium*, including even its remarkable rediscovery of the charismatic dimension of the Church.

Dulles contends that, while Newman would have 'applauded' one of the Council's 'two principal goals', *ressourcement*, he would have been 'cautious' about its other goal, *aggiornamento* or the updating of the Church. Here we need to distinguish between the conservative Anglican Newman and the comparatively liberal

Catholic Newman. It is perfectly true that as an Anglican Newman fought as a Tory against the threatened interference of the reforming Whig government in the affairs of the Church of England. And it is also true that he supported the establishment of the Church of England, although only as a necessary evil, because he feared the heretical innovations that a self-governing Church might introduce if the Evangelicals or Liberals won control of the Church. But as a Catholic, Newman became convinced, at least by the 1860s, that the establishment of Catholicism as the state religion was anachronistic and harmful to the Church's interests. Consequently, Dulles is surely too cautious when he says that Newman 'might have come to agree' with Vatican II's 'preference for disestablishment' of the Church in Catholic countries. In fact, Newman was extremely radical for his day in advocating the loss of the papacy's temporal power – a position that got him into trouble with the Church authorities for whom the temporal power was practically an article of faith. He also saw that the refusal to grant religious freedom to non-Catholics in Catholic countries was not only inconsistent with the Catholic demand for freedom in Protestant countries but also impractical and indeed counterproductive in a modern, increasingly pluralist world. I agree with Dulles's judgment that Newman 'would probably have been disappointed' by Vatican II's call for 'adaptation to the modern world', but only insofar as *aggiornamento* was interpreted in accordance with the liberal, secularising so-called 'Spirit of Vatican II'. And while he would have generally welcomed the Constitution on the Modern World, I think it is certainly true that he would have been suspicious of a certain optimism reflecting the climate of the 1960s.

Apart from these slight reservations concerning Dulles's concluding remarks in his final chapter, this book is to be highly commended as a lucid, perceptive, and reliable introduction to Newman's theology, particularly in its relation to the teaching of the Second Vatican Council. It admirably fills a surprising gap in Newman studies.

Ian Ker

Preface

While I cannot claim to be a Newman expert in the sense that Father Ian Ker and many others surely are, I have been reading Newman over many decades and have been greatly influenced by his method and teaching. The task of rereading works of Newman that I have long cherished, and delving into some of his less familiar works, has been for me both educational and enjoyable.

Initially I had some doubts about the utility of a volume such as this. Many hundreds of volumes on Newman weigh down the shelves of our libraries, and the quantity increases year by year. But most of these studies, I found, fall into one of three categories. Many are primarily biographical. Others deal with specific aspects of Newman's thought, such as his views on Christology, ecclesiology, apologetics, and the university. Still others are collections of essays on selected themes from Newman. I did not find a volume that strives, as I do here, to survey Newman's teaching about the classical theological questions in a comprehensive and systematic way. In view of the paucity of studies of this kind, there is room, I suspect, for another that attempts to be both expository and critical. As is apparent from my last chapter, I turn to the Second Vatican Council as a primary point of reference in my critical evaluation.

I could not have completed this work without assistance from many quarters. In addition to Brian Davies himself, the Reverend Robert P. Imbelli of Boston College and the Reverend John T. Ford, C.S.C., of The Catholic University of America have kindly read the entire manuscript in draft form and have offered many valuable suggestions for improvement. The Reverend Thomas L. Sheridan, S.J., of St. Peter's College, Jersey City, obligingly reviewed the chapter on Justification. My assistant, Dr. Anne-Marie Kirmse, O.P., together with Mrs. Maureen Noone, has given invaluable help, especially in correcting the proofs and in composing the index. To all these persons I extend my heartfelt gratitude.

Avery Cardinal Dulles, S.J.

Fordham University
August 11, 2002
112th anniversary of Newman's death

Abbreviations

Apol.	*Apologia pro Vita Sua*
Arians	*The Arians of the Fourth Century*
CF	*On Consulting the Faithful in the Matters of Doctrine*
Dev.	*An Essay on the Development of Christian Doctrine*
Diff.	*Certain Difficulties Felt by Anglicans in Catholic Teaching*
	Volume 1: *Twelve Lectures Addressed to the Anglican Party of 1833*
	Volume 2: *Letter to Pusey and Letter to the Duke of Norfolk*
Disc.	*Discussions and Arguments*
Discourses	*Discourses to Mixed Congregations*
Essays	*Essays Critical and Historical*, 2 vols.
GA	*An Essay in Aid of a Grammar of Assent*
Idea	*The Idea of a University Defined and Illustrated*
JHN	John Henry Newman
LD	*The Letters and Diaries of John Henry Newman*
LJ	*Lectures on Justification*
Miracles	*Two Essays on Biblical and Ecclesiastical Miracles*
OUS	*Fifteen Sermons Preached before the University of Oxford*
PPS	*Parochial and Plain Sermons*, One-Volume Edition
Sermons	*Sermons Preached on Various Occasions*
SSD	*Sermons Bearing on the Subjects of the Day*
VM	*The Via Media of the Anglican Church*
	Volume 1: *Lectures on the Prophetical Office of the Church*
	Volume 2: *Occasional Letters and Tracts*

1

Newman's pilgrimage of faith

Formative years

Because he kept such complete diaries, wrote so many letters, and composed such detailed autobiographical memoirs, the events of Newman's life are easily accessible. Dozens of solid biographies, short and long, have been published. Since this book is concerned with Newman's thought, I shall offer only a bare sketch of his life. But the main facts cannot be neglected because most of Newman's writings were occasional pieces, bound up with the vicissitudes of his own career.

John Henry Newman was born in London on February 21, 1801, the eldest of six children – three boys and three girls. His father was a moderately successful banker until his fortunes began to decline in 1814. His mother was of French Huguenot stock. His maternal grandmother took a special interest in the boy's religious education, instilling in him what he was later to describe as Bible religion. 'I was brought up as a child,' he writes, 'to take great delight in reading the Bible.' And he adds: 'Of course I had perfect knowledge of my catechism.' But he admits[1] that he had no formal religious convictions until he was fifteen.[1]

At the age of seven, Newman was sent away to boarding school at Ealing, where he received an excellent foundation in Latin and literature. As a young adolescent he began to entertain religious doubts as a result of reading Enlightenment authors such as Thomas Paine, David Hume, and perhaps Voltaire. A classics teacher at the school, the Rev. Walter Mayers, saved his faith and converted him to a kind of Calvinistic Evangelicalism by handing him books that would have a lasting effect on his religious attitudes.

Newman's response to the challenge of Enlightenment rationalism brought him beyond his childhood fantasies and the empty formalism of biblical religion. Mayers and the Calvinist authors gave him a firm conviction of the truth contained in Holy Scripture and the ancient creeds. The writings of Thomas Scott, in particular, inspired him with a strong faith in the Trinity and a realization of the overriding importance of holiness. He would always retain a keen sense of the immediate presence of God and of his moral accountability. Although he would later move beyond some of the Evangelical distinctives he held at this time, he remained lastingly committed to what he later described as the 'great and burning truths' of the gospel that he had learned as a boy.[2]

Strengthened by his first conversion, Newman enrolled as a student at Trinity College, Oxford, to which he moved in the Spring of 1817. There he spent the next three years deepening his knowledge of mathematics and the Greek and Latin classics. He also studied Bacon, Locke, and Gibbon, and became an avid reader of Walter Scott's novels. For recreation he took solitary walks and played the violin, abstaining from rowdy student parties. All the while he remained in close touch with Walter Mayers as his spiritual guide.

Although he was expected to pass his examinations in December 1820 with high honors, he suffered a nervous collapse and did poorly. But he continued to read and in April 1822, contrary to all expectation, won a fellowship at Oriel College. For the next decade he moved within a cluster of brilliant intellectuals heavily concerned with theological questions. Richard Whately, in particular, trained him to think and speak with a precision governed by Aristotle's logic, and weaned him from his rather emotional Evangelicalism. Although Newman always felt indebted to Whately, he later came to feel that Whately's religion was too cold and intellectualistic.

As a young deacon (1824) and priest (1825) of the Church of England, Newman began to serve in the parish of St. Clement. Edward Hawkins, one of the Oriel fellows, helped him with his early sermons and convinced him that he was unrealistic and judgmental in the standards he set for the laity. Hawkins also taught him to have a high regard for tradition and to work within the visible Church. In 1826, when he was appointed a tutor, Newman resigned his curacy at St. Clement's and took Hawkins's place as Vicar of the University Church of St. Mary the Virgin. But soon after Hawkins became Provost, he and Newman sharply disagreed about the proper role of tutors. Newman, unlike Hawkins, believed that as tutor he should care for the spiritual as well as the intellectual development of his charges. When relieved of his duties as tutor in 1831, he found more time for writing and research.

As a young Anglican priest Newman conducted a long correspondence with his youngest brother, Charles, who was wrestling with difficulties against faith. In these letters he began to formulate his ideas on faith and reason and his theory of apologetics. The evidence for Christianity, he maintained, 'depends a great deal on *moral feeling*.' The rejection of Christianity therefore arises 'from a fault of the *heart*, not of the *intellect*.'[3]

In the later 1820s Newman became increasingly identified with a circle of high-church Anglicans, including John Keble, Edward Pusey, and Richard Hurrell Froude. At Newman's request, Keble obtained for him in Germany a good collection of patristic writings, which he began to read systematically in 1827, beginning with the Apostolic Fathers. This project led to his first book. Asked to write a history of the councils, he became so fascinated with Nicaea that he ended up writing *The Arians of the Fourth Century* (published 1833). This book reflects the author's enthusiasm for the Alexandrian school, which looked upon the visible world as a dim reflection of a higher world to which the human mind is unequal. It traces the heresies of Arius to the influence of the school of Antioch. The book may be read as an allegory of the Oxford of Newman's day: the Alexandrians represent the Oxonian Platonists, whom Newman supports; his attacks on Antioch are disguised censures of the rationalists of contemporary Oxford. The book is of lasting interest not so much as history but because it broaches various themes that Newman would develop in later works: the sacramentality of the universe, oral tradition as a supplement to Scripture, and the *disciplina arcani* (the withholding from the people of certain exalted truths that they are not yet prepared to accept or understand).

After sending the manuscript to his publisher in 1832, Newman made a significant voyage to the Mediterranean with his friend Hurrell Froude and Froude's father. They spent time in Malta, Greece, Corfu, Naples, and Rome, where they had an interview with the future Cardinal Nicholas Wiseman, Rector of the English College. He and Froude were impressed by Wiseman's personal charm but taken aback by his doctrinal intransigence.

When the Froudes returned to England, Newman parted with them. He hired a servant named Gennaro in Naples and journeyed to Sicily, where he fell seriously ill and feared that he would die from what appears to have been typhoid fever. But he regained his health, took a ship across the Mediterranean to Marseilles, and traveled by coach through France on his way back to England. When becalmed at sea in the Straits of Bonifacio, he penned his most famous hymn, which begins: 'Lead, kindly light, amid the encircling gloom . . .' Read in retrospect, the hymn seems prophetic of Newman's future steps.

Although Newman and the Froudes were repelled by the squalor and superstition of Italian Catholicism, they also received more positive impressions. Already favorable to the rule of clerical celibacy, which they regarded as apostolic, they were struck by the devoutness of the Roman seminarians. In his solitary days in Sicily, Newman developed tender feelings toward the Church of Rome even while his reason was still against it. In his *Apologia* he recalls:

> Then, when I was abroad, the sight of so many great places, venerable shrines, and noble churches, much impressed my imagination. And my heart was touched also. Making an expedition on foot across some wild country in Sicily, at six in the morning, I came upon a small church; I heard voices, and I looked in. It was crowded, and the congregation was singing. Of course it was the mass, though I did not know it at the time. And in my dreary days at Palermo, I was not ungrateful for the comfort which I had received in frequenting the churches; nor did I ever forget it.[4]

While waiting for a ship at Palermo, Newman expressed in verse his attraction to the popular religion that he found in Italy and the sense of awe and mystery that Catholic worship was able to impart:

> Oh that thy creed were sound!
> For thou dost soothe the heart, Thou Church of Rome,
> By thy unwearied watch and varied round
> Of service, in thy Saviour's holy home.[5]

He goes on in this poem to make a moving allusion to the parable of the Good Samaritan. While pining for home, he writes, he was feeling weak and faint 'when comes a foe, my wounds with oil and wine to tend.' The practical charity that he found among Italian Catholics left a deep impression upon him.

The Oxford Movement

Newman returned to England to enter the fray of what came to be called the 'Oxford Movement.' The Movement was launched, in Newman's opinion, by Keble's sermon, 'National Apostasy,' which he was able to hear on July 14, 1833, several days after his arrival at Oxford.[6] He shared Keble's detestation of theological liberalism and of the Erastianism of the Anglican settlement – the Church's abject dependence on the civil government. The Movement, however, gradually took on a larger agenda – to reassert the essentially Catholic identity of the Church of England, purging it of its Protestant elements. For the next ten years Newman became the de facto leader of this Movement, working closely with Keble, Pusey, and, until his premature death in 1836, Froude. The principal weapon of this struggle was a series of pamphlets, *Tracts for the Times*, launched in 1833. The first of the Tracts, composed by Newman himself, was on Apostolic Succession in the ministry.

The Movement sought to vindicate the standing of the Church of England within Catholic Christianity, as a kind of sister church of Rome and Greece. The Anglo-Catholics depicted the English church as a *via media* between the relative poverty of Protestantism and the excesses of Romanism. In a series of *Lectures on the Prophetical Office of the Church*, published in 1836, Newman made a distinction between episcopal tradition, which he regarded as binding and common to the Catholic churches, and prophetic tradition, which was worthy of reverence but not in all respects binding. Rome and Canterbury, he argued, were at one regarding the teachings of the episcopal tradition, but they had relatively minor differences in the sphere of prophetic tradition.

In another series of lectures, dealing with the doctrine of justification, published in 1838, Newman sought to stake out a middle path between the Protestant doctrine of justification by a divine decree, imputing to the sinner the merits of Christ, and the Catholic doctrine, which identified justification with the infusion of sanctifying grace. Newman achieved a kind of mediation by holding that justification consists in the bestowal of the very person of the Holy Spirit. Justification, so conceived, is neither imputed nor inherent, but 'adherent.' This view, Newman maintained, was in line with the teaching of the Anglican formularies on justification by faith.

During the late 1830s Newman gained a large and enthusiastic following, especially among Oxford students, who flocked to his sermons in the Church of St. Mary the Virgin. Through his writings he became a national figure. But the more he and Pusey pressed their opposition to Protestantism, the more hostility they excited. They repeatedly had to defend themselves against accusations of being crypto-Romanists.

Several of Newman's Tracts gave grounds for suspecting that he was gravitating toward Rome; for example, Tract 75 on the Latin Breviary; Tract 85, on Scripture in Relation to the Catholic Creed, and especially Tract 90, in which he tried to prove that the Thirty-nine Articles were susceptible of a Catholic interpretation. In this last Tract, published in February 1841, Newman seemed to defend the teaching of the Council of Trent on the Mass as a sacrifice, though he continued to differ from Rome on issues such as Transubstantiation, the cult of the Blessed Virgin Mary, the invocation of saints, and Purgatory.

Tract 90 was greeted with a storm of indignation from Anglican bishops and from the heads of colleges at Oxford. To head off an official condemnation, Newman agreed to suspend the Tracts. From this point his influence in the Church of England went into steep decline. His ecclesial allegiance was further strained in 1841 when the Archbishop of Canterbury made an agreement with the Prussian minister in London to erect a joint bishopric in Jerusalem that would be held alternately by English and Prussian bishops and would minister to Anglicans, Lutherans, and Calvinists alike. Regarding this scheme as an endorsement of heresy, Newman wrote a formal letter of protest, which he sent to the Archbishop of Canterbury and to his own bishop of Oxford.

Retiring to quasi-monastic seclusion in the nearby village of Littlemore, Newman continued his patristic studies. In 1842 he published translations of *Select Treatises of St. Athanasius*; he also translated a volume from Claude Fleury's *Ecclesiastical History* dealing with the Council of Constantinople of 381 and subsequent developments. His historical studies disclosed striking analogies that told against the soundness of the *via media*. For example, he had to recognize that truth was not on the side of the Semi-Arians who tried to find a middle path between Arianism and Nicene orthodoxy. Again, he found that the moderate Monophysites in the fifth century sought in vain to find a compromise between the heresy of Eutyches and the orthodoxy expressed in Leo I's tome accepted by the Council of Chalcedon. Newman began to sense that

Anglo-Catholicism was all too reminiscent of these false mediations. The widespread rejection of his efforts by fellow-Anglicans convinced him, in addition, that the *via media* was a mere theory, a 'paper church' as he put it, rather than a real religion. Suspecting that Rome might be right after all, Newman in September 1843 resigned as vicar of St. Mary's Church.

The true Church, in Newman's view, must be one, holy, catholic, and apostolic, as stated in the Nicene-Constantinopolitan creed. Rome, no doubt, had the advantage over Canterbury with regard to catholicity; but apostolicity, he still believed, was better realized in the Church of England. Rome seemed to have deviated from the early Church by accepting medieval and modern accretions that did not belong to the apostolic deposit of faith. But this point was not easy to prove. The Church of England, unlike biblicist Protestantism, accepted the creeds and councils of Christian antiquity, which went beyond the plain meaning of Scripture. Anyone who admitted the obligatory force of the dogmas of the early centuries had to explain why the later Roman dogmas could not likewise be valid explications of the apostolic faith.

Conversion to Rome

The last of Newman's Oxford University Sermons, preached in February 1843, dealt with doctrinal development. It shows his conviction, firm by now, that doctrine does develop as the Holy Spirit assists the Church to grasp the truth implicit in the apostolic deposit. But he still needed a criterion for discerning between true and false developments. This was the crucial issue treated in Newman's great *Essay on the Development of Christian Doctrine*, composed in the years 1844–5. In writing it he answered his own objections to Roman doctrines such as papal supremacy, Purgatory, the cultus of the Blessed Virgin, and the invocation of saints. These doctrines, he now recognized, had developed logically and organically from the tradition of the early Church. Tridentine Catholicism, therefore, could be seen as the authentic heir of the Church of the Fathers. If Athanasius and Ambrose were to return to the world today, Newman believed, they would recognize the Church of Rome as their own. Once he had arrived at this realization, Newman left his *Essay* incomplete. He contacted the Italian Passionist priest, Dominic Barberi, who was at the time preaching a mission in Oxfordshire, and made his submission to Rome on October 9, 1845.

Bishop Nicholas Wiseman, who was by now vicar apostolic in England, obtained for Newman and several convert friends a residence near Birmingham, which Newman rechristened 'Maryvale.' The party moved there from Littlemore in February 1846. In September Newman and Ambrose St. John departed for Rome to study for the Catholic priesthood at the College of the Propaganda. During his Roman sojourn Newman drew up plans for establishing an English Oratory in the spirit of St. Philip Neri, who had founded the Congregation of the Oratory in the sixteenth century. Newman also found time to write a novel, *Loss and Gain*, in which the hero is an Oxford undergraduate who converts to Roman Catholicism. In this book Newman amused himself and his readers by satirical pen sketches of tutors and students representing the various religious groups at Oxford: High Church, Low Church, and Liberal.

While at Rome Newman also exerted himself to defend his *Essay on Development*, which was under attack for seeming to concede that the orthodox doctrine of the Trinity was not held in the first three centuries, thereby giving aid and comfort to the Unitarians. Newman had good reason to fear that the book would be placed on the Index of Forbidden Books.

Trials as a Catholic

Newman returned to England in December 1847, stopping on the way at Munich, where he met the church historian Ignaz von Döllinger. Back in Maryvale, he found himself severely taxed by problems of finance and administration in his new role as Superior of the Oratory. He moved the Oratory first to Birmingham in 1849 and then to nearby Edgbaston in 1850. He dispatched Frederick W. Faber and several other colleagues to establish a new Oratory in London, where they achieved great success with the help of several wealthy benefactors. Relations between the two English Oratories were a constant source of friction. Faber's enthusiasm for Italian baroque Catholicism irritated Newman, who preferred a sober piety, more attuned to the English temperament. In 1855 Faber, without consulting Newman, asked Rome for a dispensation from the common rule regarding the hearing of nuns' confessions. In the following year Newman made a trip to Rome to obtain autonomy for each of the Oratories. Never inclined to forget injuries, Newman spurned Faber's efforts to achieve reconciliation and remained unforgiving until the latter's death in September 1863.

Newman was much in demand as a lecturer and controversialist.

In a series of twelve *Lectures on Certain Difficulties Felt by Anglicans in Submitting to the Catholic Church*, delivered in the London Oratory in the Spring of 1850, he showed his capacity to be aggressively polemical, like Faber himself, to the dismay of his former Anglican constituency.

In September 1850 Pope Pius IX restored the Catholic hierarchy in England, naming Wiseman Cardinal Archbishop of Westminster. The event precipitated a burst of no-Popery that Newman felt compelled to address. In Birmingham during the summer of 1851 he gave a set of lectures *On the Present Position of Catholics in England*, brilliantly defending the Catholic Church against the popular prejudices of the day. In several paragraphs he attacked the profligacy of an ex-Dominican friar, Dr. Giovanni Achilli, who was traveling about England with lurid tales about the abuses of Catholicism. Achilli sued Newman for libel. Because of delays in gathering the necessary evidence, Newman was convicted and sentenced to pay a fine of £100. Collections were taken up by Catholics in the United States and elsewhere, which more than sufficed to defray the expense of the trial. From the excess Newman was able to finance part of the handsome church he built in Dublin.

Newman's association with Dublin began in April 1851, when Archbishop Paul Cullen of Armagh asked him to take the lead in founding a Catholic University of Ireland. Because of conflicts among the Irish bishops, difficulties in recruiting faculty, and the lack of a suitable student body in Ireland, the venture fell short of expectations. After being formally installed as Rector in June 1854, Newman resigned in February 1858. Trying though this episode was, it provided the occasion for one of Newman's finest books, *The Idea of a University*, published in 1873. This book includes Newman's nine original *Discourses on the Scope and Nature of University Education*, delivered in Dublin in 1852 and published in book form in 1853, together with a collection of *Lectures and Essays on University Subjects* originally published in 1859. The *Idea* is generally recognized as a masterful presentation of the classical theory of a liberal education, perfected in the light of Christian revelation.

While in Dublin in 1855 Newman completed his novel *Callista*, which he had begun in the Spring of 1848. The heroine is a beautiful and virtuous pagan girl who comes to realize the inadequacy of paganism and converts to Christianity in North Africa in time to be martyred in the Decian persecution. The mobs who call for the death of Christians are moved by anti-Catholic prejudices reminiscent of those Newman witnessed in England when the Catholic hierarchy was reestablished in 1850.

Still another drain on Newman's time and energies was the project for a new translation of the Bible. The idea was proposed by Cardinal Wiseman and accepted by the English bishops. In September 1857 Newman agreed to supervise the translation. He gathered a team of scholars and began work on a preface, when it became known that the United States hierarchy had commissioned Archbishop Francis Kenrick to do a new translation of the Vulgate. Because the English bishops never decided how to react to this news, the project dragged on for several years before it was called off.

The most serious setback of these years was the affair of *The Rambler*, a Catholic journal of opinion founded by a lay convert named John Moore Capes in 1848 and then directed from 1858 by another lay convert, Richard Simpson. The bishops found *The Rambler* too liberal and too critical of authority, particularly when Sir John Acton, the chief proprietor of the review, made it an organ for the liberal views of Döllinger. At the request of William Ullathorne, Bishop of Birmingham, Newman took over the editorship in the Spring of 1859. In the July issue he published his own article 'On Consulting the Faithful in Matters of Doctrine,' in which he maintained that the hierarchy in the fourth century had failed to oppose Arianism, with the result that Nicene orthodoxy was predominantly maintained by the laity. After a prominent seminary professor had denounced the article, Bishop Thomas Brown of Newport delated Newman to the Holy See for heresy. Because of a failure of communications, Newman was never informed about the precise difficulties that Rome found with his article. For that reason he failed to reply to Rome and remained for some years under a cloud of suspicion. Newman, for his part, became resentful of the Roman curia, and especially of the Congregation for the Propagation of the Faith, which was doubtful of his orthodoxy.

For the next few years Newman attempted in vain to mediate between the conservative hierarchy and the liberal faction of the laity, personified by Lord Acton. A burning issue at the time was whether the pope needed to retain his temporal power, which was being threatened by the unification of Italy. Newman tended to agree with Acton that the papacy could successfully pursue its spiritual mission without holding on to the Papal States. Henry Edward Manning, who succeeded Wiseman as Archbishop of

Westminster in 1865, regarded Newman as deficient in loyalty to the Holy See. The tension between these two great leaders was to be an additional burden on Newman for the rest of his life.

During the early 1860s it was widely rumored that Newman, disillusioned by his experiences in the Catholic Church, would return to the Church of England. Newman indignantly denied that he had the slightest thought of doing so. An opportunity for him to vindicate his allegiance to Rome came in the form of another attack upon him. In January 1864 the Protestant novelist Charles Kingsley published an article in which he charged that Newman, like other members of the Roman clergy, had little regard for truth. Newman, after consulting his lawyers, demanded a retraction. Failing to obtain a satisfactory apology, he wrote, under great pressure, a series of seven pamphlets published weekly from April 21 to June 2. Omitting two directly controversial pamphlets, he then reprinted the remaining five as a history of his religious opinions under the title *Apologia pro vita sua*. After tracing in four chapters his journey to full communion with Rome, he presented, in the fifth, his grounds for holding the truth of the Catholic faith. The book ranks with Augustine's *Confessions* among the most impressive spiritual autobiographies of all time.

Vindication and years of tranquillity

After the publication of the *Apologia* in 1865, Newman began to taste success in his career as a Catholic. The vast majority of English Catholic clergy and many Anglicans considered that he had successfully cleared his name. In the same year Newman published a long poem about Purgatory, *The Dream of Gerontius*, which won the admiration of many readers, especially for several hymns contained in it. Early in 1866, replying to Edward Pusey's somewhat polemical *Eirenicon*, he published a book-length 'Letter to the Reverend E. B. Pusey,' in which he defended the Catholic veneration of the Blessed Virgin as consonant with patristic Christianity.

In 1866, during a vacation in Switzerland with Ambrose St. John, Newman conceived the outline of his next major work, the *Essay in Aid of a Grammar of Assent*. His desire to write this book was one of his reasons for declining the invitations of several bishops to come to the Vatican Council as a theological expert. The *Grammar of Assent*, published in 1870, is Newman's most mature and thorough exposition of his theory of knowledge. The main intent of the book is to respond to 'evidentialists' such as John Locke, who contended that it was morally wrong to proffer an assent firmer than the weight of the evidence warranted. In responding to Locke, Newman hoped to facilitate the path to religious belief and solve the objections of friends like William Froude, the skeptical brother of his deceased friend Hurrell Froude.

Like the Oxford University sermons on faith and reason, the *Grammar* exhibits Newman's distrust of deductive reason. The results of inference for him depend chiefly on the presuppositions with which one begins. Certitude, he believes, is not achieved by syllogistic argument because in such cases the conclusion is held only conditionally, insofar as it follows from the premises. Newman begins not with universal propositions but with concrete experiences in which the whole person is involved. By amassing such experiences one acquires antecedent expectations that make it possible to reach certain judgments in the absence of rigorous demonstration. In the last chapter Newman contends that his principles can account for the conversion of the Roman Empire, as Edward Gibbon's explanation could not.

The *Grammar of Assent* is a highly original work. It has injected into the philosophical lexicon terms such as real and notional assent, the illative sense, and convergent probabilities. The book abounds in apt illustrations from many departments of knowledge, such as mathematics, military science, law, history, and literary criticism. It also takes account of commonsense judgments such as those of the weather-wise farmer. By situating religious knowledge in this broad context Newman gives a solid epistemological backing for his previous ventures in apologetics.

While completing his *Grammar* Newman was anxiously watching the preparations for the Vatican Council and the course of the Council itself. Although he personally believed that the pope could under certain circumstances teach infallibly, he feared that the proclamation of papal infallibility as a dogma would place unnecessary barriers in the way of people attracted to Catholic Christianity. He particularly dreaded the machinations of what he called, in a private letter to Bishop Ullathorne, an 'aggressive insolent faction' – a term that apparently referred to theologians such as Louis Veuillot and William George Ward, if not to Archbishop Manning. When the dogma was defined on July 18, 1870, Newman was relieved to find that the definition was moderately framed and did not embody the theses of extravagant papalists.

For several years after the Council Newman made no public utterance about his acceptance of its definitions. Noting that a relatively large number of bishops belonging to the minority absented themselves from the final vote on infallibility, he waited to see whether they would submit. When they did so, Newman was satisfied that the definition registered the consensus of the episcopate as a whole. In private letters he tried to reconcile friends like Acton to the new dogma.

In 1874 the former Prime Minister William E. Gladstone published an attack on the Vatican Decrees, largely inspired by Döllinger's hostile interpretation of them, which Acton was propagating in England. In response to the urging of many friends, Newman took up the pen to respond to Gladstone and defend the record of Pius IX and of the Council. In his *Letter to the Duke of Norfolk*, completed in December 1874, Newman gave a deliberately minimalist interpretation to the Syllabus of Errors of 1864 and the Vatican Council's teaching on papal primacy and infallibility. With his customary brilliance he argued that there could be no collision between personal conscience and infallible Church teaching. In response to objections from history, such as those raised by Döllinger, he maintained that history cannot prove either the truth or the falsity of religious doctrines. In his interpretation of the Vatican Council Newman relied heavily on a previous work by Bishop Joseph Fessler, the Secretary General of the Council, which Ambrose St. John had hastily translated from the German.

Once again, Newman's work was enthusiastically acclaimed, especially by the British Catholic community. Only a few extreme members of the Ultramontane party, such as the new Prefect of the Roman Propaganda, Cardinal Alessandro Franchi, privately expressed dissatisfaction. The English bishops, including Manning and Ullathorne, dissuaded Cardinal Franchi from issuing a censure.

Since 1871 Newman had begun republishing his earlier works for a uniform edition. The *Lectures on the Prophetical Office* presented a particular problem, because Newman had disavowed the central thesis of the book when he became a Catholic. In reissuing the book in 1876 as part of a two-volume work entitled *The Via Media of the Anglican Church*, Newman added a lengthy Preface in which he tried to explain that corruptions in the Church (which admittedly existed) are not due to faulty theology or doctrinal error but to the occasional excesses of popular devotion and of autocratic rule. The prophetic office, he argued, is only one of the three offices of the Church, alongside of the priestly and regal. These offices are exercised by relatively independent constituencies in the Church – the prophetic by theologians, the priestly by the faithful and their pastors, and the regal by the pope and his curia. Interestingly enough, Newman seemed to give priority to the theologians over the popes and pastors, and to blame abuses on the latter two classes. Yet he admitted that theologians can be too doctrinaire and may need to be held in check by the other two offices. The new Preface, although it seemed to have somewhat dangerous implications, was little noticed at the time, and provoked no hostile reactions, even in Rome.

At this point in his career Newman began to receive many tributes. In 1878 he was named an honorary fellow of Trinity College, Oxford, the first person ever to be so named. In May 1879 he received a far greater honor, when Pope Leo XIII elevated him to the rank of cardinal. He went to Rome to receive the official notice (the *biglietto*) and the cardinal's hat. In a speech delivered at the reception of the *biglietto* Newman maintained the unifying theme of his career had been opposition to liberalism – a term by which he meant approximately what many today would describe as the privatization of religion and its reduction to private sentiment. On this occasion he said nothing of his habitual antipathy to autocratic power.

During the 1880s Newman continued to enjoy many testimonials of esteem and affection. As his energy diminished, his literary productivity slowed down. In 1884, however, he published in the *Contemporary Review* a significant article on the inspiration of Scripture, making use of materials he had privately penned in the early 1860s. Seeking to solve the problems arising from the historical errors in the Bible, he emphasized the relative autonomy of the human authors from the Spirit who inspires them. Inerrancy, he held, should be limited to passages bearing on the faith and not applied to historical and scientific details. When a seminary professor at Maynooth questioned the orthodoxy of Newman's position, he responded indignantly, calling attention to his status as a cardinal.

Newman also engaged in an exchange of views with the Congregationalist Andrew Fairbairn in the *Contemporary Review* for October 1886. Accused of skepticism, he replied that his doubts were not about reason itself but about fallen human nature, which frequently embraces faulty presuppositions that lead to erroneous conclusions.

In the last few years of his life Newman was afflicted by failing health and saddened by the deaths of members of his family and lifelong friends. He felt that the Catholic Movement in the Church of England was being undermined by Charles Gore's liberal Catholicism. The world as a whole seemed to Newman to be falling into simple unbelief, thus fulfilling biblical prophecies of a final apostasy. But he remained serene in his personal faith until, on August 11, 1890, he died at his beloved Oratory.

Newman's principal legacy to future generations consists in his writings on theological topics. His depth of thought, breadth of knowledge, and keen sense of history, combined with his mastery of English style, have given undying popularity to these writings. In the chapters that follow I intend to review his principal ideas and arrange them in a somewhat systematic form.

Notes

1   Newman, *Apologia pro Vita Sua* (London: Longmans, Green & Co., 1929), p. 2; hereafter abbreviated *Apol.*

2   JHN to George T. Edwards, 24 February 1887, *The Letters and Diaries of John Henry Newman*, 31 vols. (London: Nelson, 1961–72, Oxford: Clarendon, 1977–), vol. 31, pp. 189; hereafter abbreviated *LD.*

3   *LD* vol. 1, pp. 214, 219.

4   *Apol.*, pp. 53–4.

5   Newman, *Verses on Various Occasions* (London: Longmans, Green & Co., 1983), p. 153.

6   Keble's sermon seems not to have made any great impression except on Newman himself, who extolled it in his *Apologia*. In his *Newman and His Age* (London: Darton, Longman & Todd, 1990), Sheridan Gilley writes of the sermon: 'Its reputation is a singular instance of Newman's ability to give a heightened quality to events in a drama in which his was one of the principal roles' (p. 111).

2

Redemption, justification, and sanctification

Christ the Redeemer

Newman wrote no monograph on Christology and was sometimes accused of neglecting the person of the Redeemer.[1] But, as Roderick Strange has shown, a loving faith in Christ lay at the root of all his theology, including his thinking on the Church and the sacraments, which were important to him as instruments through which Christ acts and as reflections through which Christ could be encountered. A fairly complete Christology can be gleaned from Newman's sermons, his book on justification, his commentaries on Athanasius, and his letters and meditations. That Christology deliberately avoids originality. Adamantly orthodox, it is in perfect accord with the teaching of Chalcedon and dependent in many ways on the Alexandrian Fathers, especially Athanasius and Cyril. With these Fathers Newman grounds his Christology in the doctrine of the Trinity. Eternally begotten from the Father, Christ is qualified to be head of all creation (Col. 1:15–17; cf. Pr. 8:22).[2]

For Newman it is axiomatic that Jesus Christ is a single person subsisting in two complete natures, divine and human. The divine has priority, because the divine person assumed the human nature; the human could not assume the divine. As a person, Christ was divine, not human. His humanity was 'an instrument of His purposes, not an agent in the work.'[3]

16

The Incarnation, for Newman, was 'the central truth of the gospel.'[4] The hypostatic union was a gift far excelling any grace that may raise creatures to participate in the divine life. In his famous hymn, 'Praise to the Holiest in the Height,' Newman expresses this excellence poetically:

O wisest love! that flesh and blood
Which did in Adam fail,
Should strive afresh against the foe,
Should strive and should prevail;

And that a higher gift than grace
Should flesh and blood refine,
God's Presence and His very Self,
and Essence all-divine.[5]

The Word became incarnate not simply to rescue mankind from its state of sin but even more to elevate it to communion with the divine. Here again, Newman confesses his debt to Athanasius:

The sanctification, or rather the deification of the nature of man, is one main subject of St. Athanasius's theology. Christ, in rising, raises His saints with Him to the right hand of power. They become instinct with His life, of one body with His flesh, divine sons, immortal kings, gods. He is in them, because He is in human nature; and He communicates to them that nature, deified by becoming His, that them It may deify.[6]

It had been disputed in the Middle Ages whether Christ would have become man if Adam had not sinned. If the motive of the Incarnation were simply to repair the fault of Adam, this question would have to be answered in the negative, as St. Thomas seems to have done. But Duns Scotus held for the affirmative. Newman himself leaned toward the Scotist view in this controversy. In a letter to F. W. Faber he said so distinctly, and added: 'But as I understand the Scotist view it simply is that He would have been incarnate, even had man not sinned – but when man sinned it was *for* our redemption; in *matter of fact* the end was to make satisfaction.'[7]

Following the high Christology stemming from the Alexandrian Fathers and perpetuated in much medieval theology, Newman tended to exaggerate the prerogatives of Christ's humanity. He

17

held, for instance, that Christ enjoyed the beatific vision and 'knew all things that a human soul can know' throughout his life on earth.[8] 'The Catholic doctrine,' Newman believed, is that 'from the moment of conception our Lord's human mind received from His Godhead as perfect a knowledge of all things as it has now.'[9] As perfect man, Jesus was free from sin but he voluntarily opened himself up to suffering and the other infirmities of our condition, as if he were himself contaminated by sin.[10] Preaching on 'The Humiliation of the Eternal Son,' Newman spoke at length of the obedience, temptations, and sufferings of Christ.[11] In an eloquent discourse on the 'Mental Sufferings of Our Lord in His Passion,' he explains that Christ did not use his awareness of his own innocence to protect himself from suffering the sense of sin and guilt:

> He knelt, motionless and still, while the vile and horrible fiend clad His spirit in a robe steeped in all that is hateful and heinous in human crime, which clung close round His heart, and filled His conscience, and found its way into every sense and pore of His mind, and spread over Him a moral leprosy, till He almost felt Himself to be that which He never could be, and which His foe would fain have made Him.[12]

Although Newman's rhetoric was not always restrained, as this quotation shows, he reacted against some of the extravagant rhetoric of Evangelical Christians. In a letter to George Edwards he deplored the 'irreverent, oratorical, and vulgar' use of the substitutionary sufferings of Christ to induce the sense of guilt and bring about conversion.[13] Without teaching explicitly that 'the Son of God dies as an Atoning Sacrifice,'[14] Newman held that this sacred doctrine was not 'to be put forth irreverently, but to be adored secretly.'[15]

All in all, Newman preferred to dwell on the more positive aspects of redemption. Following Athanasius and other Church Fathers, he depicted Christ as the representative head of regenerate humanity, dignifying all men and women by becoming a member of their family.[16] In his earthly life Jesus became an exemplar of every human virtue, 'a pattern of sanctity in the circumstances of His life.'[17] But the sanctifying power of Christ reaches beyond his earthly career. After dying for our sins, he rose again for our justification. The resurrection made it possible for Christ to apply to the elect the virtue of the Atonement.[18] The Apostles, Newman remarks, 'insist on the Resurrection as if it were the main doctrine of the gospel.'[19] In passages such as these Newman picks up the patristic theme of 'Christus Victor,' memorably celebrated by Gustaf Aulén.[20] By his resurrection from the dead Christ became the conqueror of Satan, sin, and death.[21]

Christ's work was not complete even with the resurrection. He had to ascend into heaven in order that he might send the Holy Spirit as the source of the new life of grace.[22] By that life we become Temples of the Holy Spirit, who dwells within us together with the Father and the Word.[23] These insights from Christology and pneumatology provide the key for rightly understanding Newman's theology of justification, especially in its mature form.

Newman and the Evangelicals

Newman's views regarding justification went through dramatic changes in the course of his career. The problem for him was never a merely theoretical one. It concerned him existentially ever since his first conversion at the age of fifteen, when he became a convinced believer thanks to the authors of the Calvinist tradition that Walter Mayers gave him to read. One of these authors, William Romaine, persuaded him that if he was conscious of an inward communion with God, he was elected to eternal glory and could not fall away from grace.[24] Another Evangelical Anglican, Thomas Scott, whom Newman especially admired, rejected the strict Calvinist doctrine of predestination to eternal damnation, but agreed that all who know that they are regenerate have the assurance that they will be preserved to eternal salvation.[25]

As an undergraduate at Trinity College Newman continued to adhere to the Evangelical party. In an unpublished manuscript of some ninety pages, dated June 1821, he declares that human nature is totally corrupted by original sin and that regeneration is necessary. Justification, he believes, cannot be effected by the sacrament of baptism but only by the good tidings of salvation, which the Christian finds in Holy Scripture and accepts in faith. The perfect righteousness of Christ is imputed to all who are justified by faith.[26]

A year or two later, in 1822 or 1823, the young Newman, now a fellow at Oriel, wrote a ten-page manuscript on holiness. Here again he asserts that baptism, whether infant or adult, does not convey regeneration, unless it be followed by a change of heart. The word of God, he writes, is the chief instrument of justification. Newman at this stage makes a sharp distinction between justification, as an instantaneous and extrinsic gift, and regeneration, as a gradual internal change leading toward complete holiness, the term toward which justification tends. By justification he means, as Thomas Sheridan puts it, an 'instantaneous imputation to man through faith of the merits of Christ whereby he is no longer regarded by God as a sinner and doomed to eternal misery, but becomes a child of God and an heir of heaven.'[27] Justification, he believes, is completely gratuitous and leads inevitably to eternal glory.

The Anglican *Via Media*

After 1822, Newman reports, his belief in the Calvinist doctrine of predestination 'gradually faded away.'[28] He came to regard the idea that some were predestined to eternal damnation as 'detestable.' He also ceased to believe that everyone who is regenerated by the grace of Christ is endowed with the gift of final perseverance.[29] In a memorandum of 1826 he wrote: 'I am almost convinced against predestination and election in the Calvinistic sense, that is, I see no proof of them from Scripture.'[30] Later as a Catholic he would make a sharp distinction between predestination to grace and predestination to glory. Predestination to grace is entirely gratuitous, but predestination to glory depends upon one's foreseen merits and thus requires good works. This view, which Newman attributes to the Jesuit School, has in his opinion become the common doctrine of the day.[31]

When he met Edward Pusey as a fellow at Oriel College, Newman was surprised that so devout and learned a Christian could believe in baptismal regeneration. But Newman's theological mentor, Edward Hawkins, induced him to reflect on the weight of the Church's tradition in favor of infant baptism and to recognize that there must be some grace attached to the rite.[32] Baptism, he concluded, must introduce the baptized into a covenant relationship with God that would entail the privileges of regeneration and adoption.[33]

As late as 1825 Newman still speaks of faith as 'the real instrument of justification,' but in explaining what he means, he depicts faith rather as a sign or evidence of justification.[34] In his final sermons at St. Clement's, in January 1826, we find him teaching that the Holy Spirit given in baptism is the principle of a change of heart. Regeneration, however, is a gradual process that only begins with baptism.[35]

In his sermons at St. Mary's, beginning in 1828, Newman breaks decisively with the Evangelical party. He now holds that the waters of baptism exert a spiritual influence and bring the baptized into the holy fellowship of the Church.[36] To be in the Church is to be in a state of justification and favor. Under the influence of Hurrell Froude, John Keble, and Edward Pusey, and with the help of his study of the Church Fathers, Newman progressively abandoned the Evangelical system in favor of a Church system, in which grace is communicated through the sacraments and rites of the visible Church.[37] This theological shift may be said to be complete by 1833.

As we have noted in connection with Christology, Newman was heavily influenced by his study of the Greek Fathers. Whereas he had previously used the term 'regeneration' to denote the gradual attainment of moral holiness, he now began to equate it with the divinization effected by the conferral of the Holy Spirit in baptism. As the new birth that makes us 'sharers in the divine nature' (1 Pet. 1:4), regeneration must be instantaneous.

The *Lectures on Justification*

As Newman entered into the Anglo-Catholic movement, he clarified his opinions on justification. In order to support the Anglican *via media* he delivered a series of thirteen lectures in the Adam de Brome chapel of the Church of St. Mary the Virgin in the spring of 1837. They were published the next year as his *Lectures on the Doctrine of Justification*.

In these lectures Newman seeks to trace a middle path between the Protestant position, which he ascribes to Luther, and the Roman position as found in the Council of Trent and its Catholic commentators. Luther emphasized the declarative aspect, asserting that God imputes to the sinner the righteousness of Christ. The Council of Trent, on the contrary, overlooked the imputative aspect and identified justification with its transformative effect, that is to say, with sanctification. Newman, inspired by the Fathers and the Anglican divines of the seventeenth century, attempts to find a mediating position that agrees with the Anglican Thirty-nine Articles and with the Edwardian Homilies that were authoritative for the Anglican tradition.

Newman's position is essentially a 'both/and.' The process, for him, begins with the action of God in bringing about justification by his declaratory word. The term 'justification' refers primarily to this action of God and only secondarily to the effect. But Newman agrees with the Catholics that the word of God is efficacious, and hence that 'justification' may be used to signify the righteousness that is imparted. Justification and regeneration, therefore, are two aspects of the same process.

Newman attributes justification to a variety of agencies, beginning with Christ and the Holy Spirit. Christ on the Cross accomplished the Atonement, and after his resurrection he applies its fruits by sending his Spirit. As Christ was the chief agent of Atonement, so the Holy Spirit is the chief agent of justification.[38]

Newman knows well that the eleventh of the Thirty-nine Articles states explicitly: 'We are saved by faith only.' As an Anglican he tries to find an acceptable interpretation of this formula, which does not seem to be to his liking. Faith, he allows, may be said to be justifying insofar as it fixes our minds on Christ and makes us receptive to his justifying action. Faith looks to Christ as the one who justifies. But Newman is concerned that the term 'faith alone,' used as a slogan, can easily lead to enthusiasm and antinomianism.[39]

To correct these aberrations, which he attributes to the Evangelical party in the Church of England, Newman goes back to what he regards as the teaching of the ancient Church. Faith, he contends, does not convey justification but receives and preserves it. Prior to baptism, faith does not yet justify. 'Faith then must not be called the new birth,' for this is not the teaching of Holy Scripture.[40]

Having disposed of the Protestant error, Newman criticizes the Roman position. He turns his fire not on any official teaching of the Church, but on certain unnamed theologians who felt obliged, in fidelity to Trent, to speak as though justification consisted exclusively in the inner sanctification and obedience that result from God's favor. This type of theology, he objects, tends to fix our minds on ourselves rather than on Jesus Christ, who is our justification. In this connection Newman expresses some reservations about the term, 'inherent righteousness.'

> If the Presence of Christ is our true righteousness, first conveyed into us by Baptism, then more sacredly and mysteriously in the Eucharist, we have really no inherent righteousness at all. What seems to be inherent, may be more properly called *adherent*, depending, as it does, wholly and absolutely upon the Divine Indwelling, not ours to keep, but as heat in a sickly person, sustained by a cause distinct from himself.[41]

In these words Newman intimates his own position. Whereas the term 'justification' refers in the first place to God's declaratory act, the reality of justification consists rather in the indwelling of the Holy Spirit, who regenerates and sanctifies. This indwelling is conferred through the external instrumentality of baptism, the sacrament by which we are incorporated into the Body of Christ and the temple of Holy Spirit.

In these lectures Newman treats faith in its cognitive aspect. He calls it 'the mind's perception or apprehension of heavenly things, arising from an instinctive trust in the divinity or truth of the external word, informing it concerning them.'[42] For adults faith is necessary for acquiring and maintaining righteousness, but does not suffice for justification unless accompanied and enlivened by the other theological virtues, especially charity. Nor does faith justify without works, which are the means by which it manifests itself. Works done prior to justification are not pleasing to God and do not justify, but works done under the influence of the indwelling Spirit are pleasing to God and meritorious, as Luther himself recognized.[43]

Summarizing his position, Newman can say: 'Justification comes *through* the sacraments; is received *by* faith; *consists* in God's inward presence; and *lives* in obedience.'[44] The emphasis clearly falls on the constitutive element, the inhabitation of the Holy Spirit.

As an objection to his own position, Newman adduces the example of Abraham, who was accounted just because of his faith even though he did not receive baptism and was not incorporated into the Body of Christ. Newman replies that Abraham lived in a different era, in which different provisions were made for justification. Ancient Israel looked forward to the coming of Christ, and had access to justification by imputation. But the same is not true in the Kingdom founded by Christ, in which the righteousness of ancient times is superseded.[45]

The *Lectures*, according to Newman, were primarily intended to set forth his positive teaching, 'offering suggestions towards ... the consolidation of a theological system.'[46] But they contain some fiercely polemical passages. Dismissing the Evangelical position, which is his principal target, Newman writes:

Away then with this modern, this private, this arbitrary, this unscriptural system, which promising liberty conspires against it; which abolishes Christian Sacraments to introduce barren and dead ordinances; and for the real participation of the Son, and justification through the Spirit, would, at the very marriage feast, feed us on shells and husks, who hunger and thirst after righteousness. It is a new gospel, unless three hundred years stand for eighteen hundred; and if men are bent on seducing us from the ancient faith, let them provide a more specious error, a more alluring sophism, a more angelic tempter, than this.[47]

Of Luther he says: 'He found Christians in bondage to their works and observances; he released them by his doctrine of faith; and he left them in bondage to their feelings.'[48]

Appraisal of the *Lectures*

In a judgment that is widely shared, Ian Ker declares that Newman's *Lectures on Justification* are 'arguably his most profound and subtle theological work.'[49] Alister McGrath calls the *Lectures* 'easily the most significant theological writing to emerge from the Oxford Movement.'[50] As the issue of justification has assumed a new centrality in ecumenical discussion, Newman's analysis is beginning to receive more attention than in the past. He felicitously combines the Protestant concern for the merits of Christ apprehended in faith with the Catholic concern for real interior transformation by grace. In a sense he transcends the difference by putting the accent on the divine indwelling – a theme always dear to Eastern theologians.

Newman develops his views in opposition to various adversaries. His criticism of Catholic positions is relatively mild. He accuses some unnamed theologians of the Counter-Reformation of identifying justification too exclusively with the created gift of sanctifying grace, thus tending to promote undue self-reliance. Even though Newman as a Catholic retracted this criticism, Catholics might do well to attend to it.[51]

The most serious difficulty raised against Newman's analysis has to do with his treatment of Luther, whom he reads as the author of the Evangelical 'experientialist' doctrine he intends to refute. Luther's position was much more complex, especially because he later turned on the 'enthusiasts' as fiercely as he had previously attacked what he took Catholics to hold.

Alister McGrath, in his comprehensive history of the doctrine of justification, makes the point that Luther does not understand 'justification by faith' to mean that man puts his trust in God, and is justified on that account. Rather, he says, 'it means that God bestows upon that man faith and grace, without his cooperation, effecting within him the real and redeeming presence of Christ as the 'righteousness of God' within him, and justifying him on *this* account.'[52] In a similar vein, Richard John Neuhaus has protested: 'If justification by faith means, as Newman suggests, a turn to the self, a reliance upon subjective feeling, and other deformations associated with what he calls 'experimental religion,' then Luther emphatically rejected justification by faith.'[53] If Neuhaus is correct, Luther was quite consistent in holding for both justification by faith and baptismal regeneration. The Protestant tradition, Neuhaus argues, later misconstrued Luther, neglecting the Catholic elements in his theology.

However that may be, Newman's own blending of justification and regeneration, and of faith, love, and divine indwelling, can serve as a model for Christians seeking to overcome the unilateralism of their traditions and recover the integral message of Scripture and tradition. Recent consensus statements, such as the ARCIC II Agreed Statement on 'Salvation and the Church' (1987)[54] and Lutheran-Catholic 'Joint Declaration' of October 31, 1999,[55] would no doubt have gratified Newman as generally consonant with his thinking. To quote Ian Ker again: 'As a theological work, the *Lectures*, although hardly eirenic in intention or tone, can now be seen to be a pioneering classic of 'ecumenical' theology.'[56]

The *Parochial and Plain Sermons*

The eight volumes of Newman's *Parochial and Plain Sermons*, preached between 1825 and 1843, by their warmly pastoral tone admirably supplement his *Lectures on Justification*. In these sermons he focuses less on justification as a declaratory act of God than on the holiness effected in believers through the indwelling of the Holy Spirit. This indwelling, for Newman, is conferred through the sacraments, and especially through baptism, which initiates us into the Body of Christ.

The first sermon in the collection bears the characteristic title, 'Holiness Necessary for Future Blessedness.' Newman takes as his text the words of Hebrews 12:14, 'Holiness, without which no man shall see the Lord.' Already in this sermon he preaches the necessity of obedience and good works, which gradually detach us from this world of sense and impress a heavenly character on our hearts. Throughout the eight volumes the themes of repentance, conversion, and obedience will continually reappear.

Late in 1834 Newman preached at St. Mary's a sermon on 'The Indwelling Spirit' in which he extols baptismal regeneration:

> This wonderful change from darkness to light, through the entrance of the Spirit into the soul, is called Regeneration, or the New Birth; a blessing which, before Christ's coming, not even Prophets and righteous men possessed, but which is now conveyed to all men freely through the Sacrament of Baptism. By nature we are children of wrath, the heart is sold under sin, possessed by evil spirits; and inherits death as its eternal portion. But by the coming of the Holy Ghost, all guilt and pollution are burned away as by fire, the devil is driven forth, sin, original and actual, is forgiven, and the whole man is consecrated to God.[57]

In another homily from this period he defines regeneration even more sharply: 'What is Regeneration? It is the gift of a new and spiritual nature, but men have, through God's blessing, obeyed and pleased him without it.' By God's appointment, he concludes, the visible Church is the minister and baptism the instrument of that new birth which we call regeneration.[58]

Newman's views on justification in his final years as an Anglican are conveniently summarized in his sermon of 1841, 'Faith the Title for Justification.'[59] The crux of the argument depends on the word 'title.' At the very beginning he asserts that 'the grace of Christ is not a mere favorable regard with which He [God] views us, a mere state of acceptance and external imputation of His merits given to faith.' He then quotes a whole series of New Testament texts that speak of inward renewal following upon baptism. His problem is to reconcile these texts with certain Pauline passages that speak of justification by faith. He achieves this reconciliation by proposing that faith gives the believer a title to be justified, but does not actually effect justification. Believers are not justified until they are joined to the Body of Christ by baptism, the instrument by which we are grafted into the Church. For this reason Peter in his Pentecost sermon called upon his hearers to be baptized for the remission of their sins and the reception of the Holy Spirit. In later chapters of Acts we learn that it was urgent for converts such as the Ethiopian eunuch, Paul, and Cornelius and his household to be baptized.

At the close of this sermon Newman grants that there are exceptional cases in which baptism is not available to a believer, for example, a catechumen who dies before being received into the

Church. Following the doctrine of the ancient Church, Newman grants that martyrdom can be counted as a substitute for sacramental baptism. He speculates that just as the saints of the Old Testament were justified without baptism, God may make some extraordinary dispensation for the salvation of others who are not in a position to obtain baptism. But Newman continues to insist that as a general principle faith cannot serve in the place of baptism. For those who have access to it, baptism is a necessary means of grace.

Catholic writings

When he wrote his first novel, *Loss and Gain*, during his Roman sojourn in 1847, Newman included a severe criticism of the Evangelical party in the Church of England, whose positions he himself had in part accepted in his youth. The novel is largely taken up with debates about religion among young tutors and students at Oxford, who liberally quote sixteenth-century sources, such as the Articles of Religion, the Homilies, and the writings of Martin Luther and Philip Melanchthon, often in Latin. A young master named Freeborn appears as the spokesman of the Evangelical point of view. At a breakfast party hosted by the Puseyite Bateman, Freeborn expresses his dislike of theology on the ground that it substitutes worthless intellectual notions for the vital truths of religion. Freeborn also dismisses the doctrine of baptismal regeneration.

> 'Faith,' said Freeborn, 'is a Divine gift, and is the instrument of our justification in God's sight. We are all by nature displeasing to Him, till He justifies us freely for Christ's sake. Faith is like a hand, appropriating personally the merits of Christ, who is our justification. Now what can we want more, or have more, than those merits? Faith, then, is everything, and does everything for us.'[60]

Freeborn then goes on to explain that faith both justifies and sanctifies. The Oxford students in the novel then engage in an involved debate about the relationship of faith to charity and good works, which Freeborn sees as necessarily flowing from it. Does faith justify even before it produces its fruits? When Charles Reding, the hero of the novel, confesses his inability to grasp the coherence of Freeborn's position, Freeborn turns to sentiment:

'Oh,' he said, 'if you really once experienced the power of faith – how it changes the heart, enlightens the eyes, gives a new spiritual taste, a new sense to the soul; if you once knew what it was to be blind, and then to see, you would not ask for definitions. Strangers need verbal descriptions, the heirs of the kingdom enjoy. Oh, if you could but be persuaded to put off high imaginations, to strip yourself of your proud self, and to *experience* in yourself the wonderful change, you would live in praise and thanksgiving, instead of argument and criticism.'[61]

This appeal to experience and feeling runs counter to Newman's intellectual and dogmatic form of religion. At no point in his career did he undergo anything resembling the sudden conversion of the heart to which the followers of Wesley customarily appealed. Newman considered that the substitution of emotion for intelligence and of individualism for tradition was destroying the status of religious faith in the ambience of the university.

When he reissued the *Lectures on Justification* as a Catholic in 1874, Newman did not feel any need to make substantive changes. His emphasis on the indwelling of the Holy Spirit is in fact quite compatible with the teaching of Trent. In his 'Advertisement' to the new edition he maintains that his position on the presence of God in the soul as the 'form' of justification is not really contrary to Trent, which spoke of grace or charity in the soul as the only formal cause of justification. He suggests that the 'one formal cause' could consist of two partial forms. The substantial presence of the Holy Spirit would be the principal or primary form, and created grace or charity the secondary form.[62]

The afterlife

Justification and sanctification, the principal foci of this chapter, are of course ordered toward the final state into which the soul enters after death. The preceding discussion therefore needs to be completed by some consideration of the end for which the present life is a preparation.

As an Anglican, Newman thought chiefly in terms of two outcomes: heaven and hell. The difference between them depended chiefly on the state of the soul. Heaven is a place of perfect happiness, but only to the holy. For the reprobate, a summons to heaven would be the greatest of punishments. 'Heaven,' writes Newman, 'would be hell to an irreligious man.'[63]

Human language, for Newman, is quite incapable of describing the glories that are to come, but the images in revelation are sufficient to kindle our longing for eternal blessedness.

> The one desire which should move us should be, first of all, that of seeing Him face to face, who is now hid from us; and next of enjoying eternal and direct communion, in and through Him, with our friends around us, whom at present we know only through the medium of sense, by precarious and partial channels, which give us little insight into their hearts.[64]

The Anglican Newman comes very close to affirming the Catholic doctrine of purgatory. In the particular judgment, he writes, we shall stand before the righteous presence of God himself, enduring his holy and searching glance.[65] That piercing glance, he says, will strip away all earthly illusions and make us confront 'the fierce and terrifying vision of our real selves, that last fiery trial of the soul before its acceptance, a spiritual agony and second death to all who are not then supported by the strength of Him who died to bring them safe through it, and in whom on earth they have believed.'[66]

In an Anglican sermon on 'The Intermediate State' Newman rejects depictions of purgatory as a place of torment, a kind of temporary hell. The faithful departed, he says, are in a state of repose and security. Then he puts the question:

> Who can tell, then, but, in God's mercy, the time of waiting between death and Christ's coming, may be profitable to those who have been His true servants here, as a time of maturing that fruit of grace, but partly formed in them in this life – a school-time of contemplation, as this world is a discipline of active service?[67]

After joining the Catholic Church Newman develops some of the same themes, combining them with an explicit acceptance of purgatory. He speaks of the eagerness with which the loving soul 'on its separation from the body, approaches the judgment-seat of its Redeemer.' It yearns to hear the Savior's voice, 'to hear Him speak, though it be to punish.'[68] In Newman's lengthy poem, *The Dream of Gerontius*, the soul of Gerontius, after enjoying a momentary vision of the Lord as judge, willingly accepts the spiritual fire by which the dross of its own sinfulness is burnt away. While suffering intensely because of its longing for Christ and its shame at having sinned, the soul experiences peace. Delivered from all fear of damnation, it is comforted by angels and assured of its final salvation. The poem eloquently conveys Newman's sense of Christ's redemptive love, the guardianship of the angels, the hatred of the demons, and the support of the prayers of the saints on earth.

Newman wrote comparatively little about hell, except to warn sinners against it. As for the eternity of damnation, he concedes that 'men of the world would shrink from a doctrine like this as impossible, and religious men answer that it is a mystery.' It reminds us that God's infinite holiness and justice lie utterly beyond human measure and understanding.[69]

In the *Grammar of Assent* Newman points out that the human mind, in this life, is utterly powerless to form a positive notion of eternity. He also alludes to the opinion that the sufferings of the damned, although eternal, might be occasionally alleviated at least for some.[70] In a note appended to the *Grammar* in 1882, he suggests that the souls in hell might experience millions of years of punishment as though they were only a passing moment. His hypothesis is very tentative, subtly argued, and deferentially submitted to the judgment of the Church.[71]

Newman's reflections on the afterlife are of continuing interest because of the author's keen psychological insight and his efforts to integrate eschatology with Christology and ecclesiology. When he speaks of the particular judgment, he never allows the reader to forget that Christ is also our merciful Redeemer. Escaping the individualism of many treatments, he gives due scope to the communion of saints. He shows how the souls undergoing judgment might be pained by the realization of their own unworthiness in relation to the sanctity of God. But he dispels the gloom usually associated with death and purification by attending to the consolations as well as the sufferings. His musings on the experience of the afterlife open up dimensions absent from most dogmatic treatments of the subject.

Notes

1   Thomas Arnold, the headmaster of Rugby school, wrote to A. P. Stanley on May 24, 1836: 'It is clear to me that Newman and his party are idolaters; they put Christ's Church and Christ's Sacraments, and Christ's ministers, in the place of Christ Himself' – text in Arthur P. Stanley, *The Life and Correspondence of Thomas Arnold, D.D.*, 2 vols. (Boston: Ticknor and Fields,

1869), vol. 2, p. 47. Roderick Strange, after quoting this passage in his *Newman and the Gospel of Christ* (Oxford: Oxford University Press, 1981), p. 1, answers the charge thoroughly in the rest of his book.

2 Strange, *Newman and the Gospel*, pp. 134–56, cites a number of texts from Athanasius that were used by Newman in his commentaries.

3 Newman, *Parochial and Plain Sermons*, one-volume edition (San Francisco: Ignatius, 1987), 6:5, p. 1215; hereafter abbreviated *PPS*. Here again, Newman echoes the language of Athanasius, who spoke of the humanity as *organon*; Strange, *Newman and the Gospel*, pp. 63–4.

4 Newman, *An Essay on the Development of Christian Doctrine* (Notre Dame, IN.: University of Notre Dame, 1989), p. 324; hereafter abbreviated *Dev.*

5 Newman, *Verses for Various Occasions* (London: Longmans, Green & Co., 1893), pp. 363–4. Some authors, mistakenly in my opinion, interpret Newman as here asserting that the indwelling of the Holy Spirit in the justified Christian is a higher gift than sanctifying grace. See, for example, Alister McGrath, *Iustitia Dei: A History of the Christian Doctrine of Justification*, 2nd edn (Cambridge: Cambridge University Press, 1998), p. 310.

6 *Dev.*, p. 140.

7 JHN to Frederick W. Faber, 9 December 1849, *The Letters and Diaries of John Henry Newman*, 31 vols. (London: Nelson,1961–72 Oxford: Clarendon, 1977–), vol. 13, p. 335; hereafter abbreviated *LD*.

8 Newman, *Select Treatises of Saint Athanasius*, 2 vols. (London: Longmans, Green & Co., 1895), vol. 2, p. 162.

9 JHN to Henry Wilberforce, 1 January 1849, *LD*, vol. 13, p. 3.

10 See Newman's sermon on 'The Incarnation,' *PPS*, 2:3, p. 245.

11 Ibid., 3:12, pp. 578–87.

12 Newman, *Discourses to Mixed Congregations* (London: Longmans, Green & Co., 1893), pp. 323–41, at pp. 336–7.

13 JHN to George T. Edwards, 24 February 1883, *LD*, vol. 30, pp.188–9.

14 *PPS*, 6:6, p. 1221.

15 Ibid., 6:7, p. 1233.

16 *Select Treatises*, vol. 2, p. 135.

17 *PPS*, 5:7, p. 1010.

18 Newman, *Lectures on Justification* (Westminster, MD.: Christian Classics, 1966), p. 206. This is a photo-offset reprint of the third edition, 1874; hereafter abbreviated *LJ*.

19 Ibid., p. 221.

20 Gustaf Aulén, *Christus Victor: An Historical Study of the Three Main Types of the Idea of Atonement*, trans. A. G. Hebert (New York: Macmillan, 1951).

21 Strange, *Newman and the Gospel*, pp. 107–9.

31

22   *LJ*, p. 206.

23   Ibid., 144.

24   John Henry Newman, *Apologia pro Vita Sua* (London: Longmans, Green & Co., 1929), p. 4. (Hereafter abbreviated *Apol.*)

25   Ibid., p. 5. On the views of Thomas Scott see Thomas Sheridan, *Newman on Justification* (Staten Island, NY: Alba House, 1967), pp. 23–34.

26   Sheridan, *Newman on Justification*, pp. 51–6.

27   Ibid., p. 64.

28   *Apol.*, p. 4.

29   Ibid., p. 6.

30   Newman, *Autobiographical Writings* (New York: Sheed & Ward, 1957), p. 208.

31   Newman, 'A Letter Addressed to His Grace the Duke of Norfolk ...,' in *Certain Difficulties Felt by Anglicans in Roman Catholic Teaching Considered*, 2 vols. (London: Longmans, Green & Co., 1910), vol. 2, pp. 175–378, at p. 336.

32   Sheridan, *Newman on Justification*, pp. 98–9.

33   Ibid., p. 102.

34   Ibid., pp. 106, 116.

35   Ibid., p. 121.

36   Ibid., pp. 153–4.

37   Ibid., p. 176.

38   *LJ*, p. 204.

39   'Enthusiasm' in the theological sense is the doctrine that God converts human beings without any created means, and thus apart from the word and the sacraments. 'Antinominianism' is the doctrine that Christians are freed from the obligation to keep the moral law.

40   *LJ*, p. 241.

41   Ibid., p. 187.

42   Ibid., p. 253.

43   Ibid., p. 301, quoting Luther's commentary on Gal. 3:10.

44   Ibid., p. 278.

45   Ibid., pp. 192–201.

46   Ibid., p. vi.

47   Ibid., p. 57.

48   Ibid., p. 340.

49   Ian Ker, *Newman the Theologian* (Notre Dame, IN: University of Notre Dame Press, 1990), p. 29.

50   McGrath, *Iustitia Dei*, p. 309.

51   Ibid., p. 190, with footnote 1.

52   McGrath, *Iustitia Dei*, p. 313. McGrath pursues the inaccuracy of Newman's interpretation of Luther in his essay 'Newman on Justification: An Evangelical Anglican Evaluation,' in Terrence Merrigan and Ian T. Ker (eds.), *Newman and the Word* (Louvain: Peeters Press, 2000), pp. 91–107.

53   Richard John Neuhaus, 'Newman, Luther, and the Unity of Christians,' *Pro Ecclesia* 6 (1997), p. 277–88, at p. 281.

54   Anglican-Roman Catholic Agreed Statement, 'Salvation and the Church,' *Origins* 16 (February 5, 1987), pp. 611–16.

55   Lutheran-Catholic Dialogue, 'Joint Declaration on the Doctrine of Justification,' *Origins* 28 (July 16, 1998), pp. 120–7.

56   Ian Ker, *John Henry Newman: A Biography* (Oxford: Clarendon, 1989), p. 157.

57   *PPS*, 2:19; pp. 366–7.

58   Ibid., 3:16, p. 623.

59   Ibid., 6:12, pp. 1272–84.

60   Newman, *Loss and Gain: The Story of a Convert* (London: Longmans, Green & Co., 1896), p. 137.

61   Ibid., p. 142.

62   *LJ*, pp. x–xii.

63   *PPS* 1:1, p. 9.

64   Ibid., 4:14, p. 866.

65   Ibid., 5:1, pp. 952–3.

66   Ibid., 1:4, p. 35.

67   Ibid., 3:25, pp. 709–21; quotation from p. 715.

68   *Discourses*, p. 81.

69   Ibid., p. 318.

70   Newman, *Essay in Aid of a Grammar of Assent* (London: Longmans, Green & Co., 1901), p. 422.

71   Ibid., n. 3, pp. 501–3.

3

Faith and reason

Throughout his career, Newman was preoccupied with the relations between faith and reason. In his early years as an Evangelical, he tended to assign priority to faith. Shortly after becoming a fellow at Oriel he found himself 'beginning to prefer intellectual excellence to moral' and used 'flippant language against the Fathers.'[1] But in his Anglo-Catholic period he overcame his incipient rationalism and returned to a stance of faith without diminishing his respect for reason.

Oxford University Sermons

The development of Newman's thought on the faith–reason relationship during his Anglo-Catholic period can conveniently be tracked in his Oxford University Sermons. The fourth of these, preached in 1831, reads like a self-criticism of his own earlier rationalism and that of Oriel 'noetics' such as Richard Whately. The sermon is directed against 'The Usurpations of Reason.' According to the testimony of Scripture, Newman contends, unlearned faith, 'establishing itself by its own inherent strength,' rules over reason as its captive.[2] The Church, he explains, has employed reason as the servant of faith but has never treated reason as an equal or a patron. He even agrees with David Hume that those who undertake to defend religion by the principles of human reason are dangerous allies or disguised enemies. Reason is at best an instrument.

In the later University Sermons we may trace a gradual upgrading of reason along with an expanding notion of reason itself. A notable shift occurs in Sermon X, 'Faith and Reason Contrasted as Habits of Mind,' preached on Epiphany Sunday, 1839. At this point Newman sees faith as a novel principle of action and reason as a critical principle of reflection. Faith, he says, must be in accord with right reason, but it does not have its source in reason.[3] In this sermon he concedes to Hume that reason is severer in its demands than faith, which is content with weaker evidence.[4] In Sermon XI, preached the following week, he explains that faith is the reasoning of a religious mind and that the act of faith is itself an exercise of reason – that is to say, of reason that outdoes itself by boldly putting its trust in evidence that seems relatively weak.[5] In Sermon XII, 'Love the Safeguard of Faith against Superstition,' preached in May, 1839, he makes a further advance. Defining reason very broadly as any process by which the mind advances from one thing to another, Newman states that reason, so understood, includes faith.[6] He recognizes, however, that reason is commonly understood as resting on grounds common to all.[7] Faith, by contrast, is 'a reasoning on presumptions; right Faith is a reasoning upon holy, devout, and enlightened presumptions.'[8] Where faith fails to rise to the standard of love, it easily falls into superstition.

In Sermon XIII Newman introduces an important distinction between explicit and implicit reason. All men, he says, reason, and have implicit reasons for holding what they do, but only those trained to be reflective can give explicit reasons. Scientific knowledge, he contends, is of such a nature that it can state its own grounds. In the sphere of religious knowledge, where the mind is seeking out the word of God, the object is too complex and the evidences are too multiple and indistinct for the mind to formulate probative arguments. Those who seek to regulate their beliefs by grounds that can be plainly exhibited in argument often fall short of fully accepting God's word.

Sermon XIV, preached in the Spring of 1841, makes distinctions between faith, wisdom, and bigotry. Faith, Newman declares, is a spontaneous exercise of reason, whereas wisdom is an orderly and mature development of thought. Faith, he says, reaches forward toward the truth; it acts boldly on slender evidence. Unlike bigotry, faith is willing to confess its own ignorance and is ever eager to learn. Bigotry makes a show of wisdom, whereas faith is content to appear foolish.

The critique of rationalism

Faith, according to the Oxford University Sermons, necessarily rests on moral and religious presuppositions. It cannot stand up unless it is rooted in a spirit of humility and openness to God's gracious gift. At many points in his career Newman attacked the spirit of rationalism, which demands that God provide stringent proofs for revelation as a condition for our acceptance of it.

In 1835 Newman composed his Tract 73, 'On the Introduction of Rationalistic Principles into Revealed Religion.'[9] Here he defines rationalism as an abuse whereby reason makes itself the standard of doctrines revealed. Faith, he holds, is an acceptance of mystery, which reason cannot reach by its own powers and can accept only on the basis of testimony. The truths of faith, being obscure and mysterious, must be treated with great reverence. The rationalist errs by taking himself, rather than the Creator, as his own center. For the rationalist faith is never more than an opinion.

In a series of seven letters to the London *Times* composed in 1841, Newman delivered a rhetorically brilliant excoriation of rationalism. Two eminent statesmen of the day, Lord Henry Brougham and Sir Robert Peel, had proposed that the claims of religion could be suitably sustained by establishing nondenominational public reading rooms for the education of the masses. The wonders of science, they contended, would arouse faith in the great Architect of the universe. Newman was not convinced. 'Deductions,' he replied, 'have no power of persuasion'; science has no religious tendency. He went on to say:

The heart is commonly reached, not through the reason but through the imagination, by means of direct impressions, by the testimony of facts and events, by history, by description. Persons influence us, voices melt us, looks subdue us, deeds inflame us. Many a man will live and die upon a dogma: no man will be a martyr for a conclusion. A conclusion is but an opinion ...

Logic makes but a sorry rhetoric with the multitude; first shoot round corners, and you may not despair of converting by a syllogism. ... To most men argument makes the point in hand only more doubtful, and considerably less impressive. After all, man is *not* a reasoning animal; he is a seeing, feeling, contemplating, acting animal. ...

Life is not long enough for a religion of inferences; we shall never have done beginning, if we determine to begin with proof. ... Life is for action. If we insist on proofs for everything, we shall never come to action: to act you must assume, and that assumption is faith. ... If we commence with scientific knowledge and argumentative proof, or lay any great stress upon it as the basis for personal Christianity, or attempt to make man moral and religious by libraries and museums, let us in consistency take chemists for our cooks, and mineralogists for our masons.[10]

Newman was not alone among his contemporaries in rejecting rationalism. Some of his friends and associates, such as John Keble, chose the path of intuitionism. Following the Cambridge Platonists of the seventeenth century, the intuitionists held that the pure of heart possess a cognitive organ that enables them to apprehend spiritual reality directly. Newman regards this position as pious but unconvincing. He is wary of appeals to spiritual experiences. We possess no faculty, he asserts, for directly perceiving the realities of faith. As Paul asserts, faith comes by hearing (Rom. 10:8). In other words, faith rests upon testimony, not upon seeing. 'As then testimony is distinct from experience, so is Faith from Reason.'[11] In a private letter of 1871 he puts this even more strongly. He imagines someone saying to him. 'To see and touch the supernatural with my soul, with its *own experience*, that is what I want to do.' Newman replies: 'Yes, it is. You wish to 'walk *not* by faith *but* by sight.' If you had *experience*, how would it be faith?'[12] Although we hope for vision in the life to come, in this life the saying of Jesus remains true: Blessed are they who have not seen and have believed (Jn 20:29).

The critique of evidentialism

In his theory of religious assent Newman was deliberately opposing evidentialism, a form of rationalism favored among empiricists, which had been in England since the seventeenth century. Evidentialism is epitomized by the dictum of John Locke, who wrote that the lover of truth will not entertain any proposition with greater assurance than the proofs it is built upon will warrant.[13] He objects to what he calls the 'surplusage of assent ... beyond the degrees of that evidence.' Reason, he holds, 'must be our last judge and guide in everything.'[14] The evidentialist school of apologetics, represented by William Paley, took up Locke's challenge and sought to prove that the truth of the Christian religion could be conclusively demonstrated by external proofs such as miracles and fulfilled prophecies. Newman, in the Oxford University Sermons and elsewhere, warns against the objectivism of the evidentialist school. He makes four main objections.

In the first place, this thesis does not account for the facts. The great majority of committed Christians, Newman declares, do not believe because the evidence has convinced them. 'If children, if the poor, if the busy, can have true Faith, yet cannot weigh evidence, evidence is not the simple foundation on which Faith is built.'[15] In his *Essay on the Development of Christian Doctrine*, Newman makes the following criticism of Locke:

> It does not seem to have struck him that such a philosophy as his cuts off from the possibility and the privilege of faith all but the educated few, all but the learned, the clear-headed, the men of practised intellects and balanced minds, men who had leisure, who had opportunities of consulting others, and kind and wise friends to whom they deferred.[16]

In this passage Newman recalls that for nearly nine years Augustine had been misled by the Manichaeans, the evidentialists of his day, into slighting the religion that had been sown in him by his parents.[17]

Secondly, Newman maintains, evidences rarely bring people to change their views. Religious minds, as a general rule, embrace the gospel because it responds to their religious needs, whereas evidences are thrown away on irreligious minds.[18]

Thirdly, revealed religion is to be accepted not simply by the intellect but by the whole person as a gracious gift from a loving God. Supposing that someone could be converted by sheer force of argument, without feeling the need or the desire of it, how would that person be the better for believing?[19]

Lastly, Newman holds that when people do accept Christianity on the basis of the evidence, they do not achieve certitude. By its very nature evidence leads not to conversion or faith but to conclusions, which stand up only as long as the arguments do. The assent to the conclusion remains conditional, for it depends on the reasons given. Persons who rely on evidence are constantly at the mercy of new arguments that might upset the conclusions to which they at present adhere.[20]

Antecedent probabilities

In considering what determines a person to accept a creed or believe a witness, Newman holds that the mind is 'mainly swayed by antecedent considerations.' It is influenced by prepossessions or, in the good sense of the word, prejudices, rather than by direct and definite proof.[21] Newman is saying, in effect, that reason does not operate in a vacuum. People react to the evidence in accordance with their previous attitudes and expectations. The testimony seems convincing to those who are previously disposed to believe it and unconvincing to others.

Turning the tables against unbelievers such as Hume, Newman points out that unbelief 'goes upon presumptions and prejudices as much as faith does, only presumptions of an opposite nature.'[22] Thus the unbeliever cannot claim to be more reasonable than the believer. But Newman at this point creates a problem for himself. His argument might seem to justify every kind of superstition or, on the other hand, skepticism, since in the end no conviction would rest on an objectively secure foundation. Why should one accept a given religious belief-system over its rivals and over irreligion?

Newman himself calls attention to the difficulty, and seeks to answer it.[23] The safeguard of faith against superstition and infidelity, he maintains, is not objective evidence but a right state of heart. We believe the message of the gospel because we have good moral presuppositions. A loving disposition of heart will cause the mind to recoil from cruelty and impurity, and to seek communion with the invisible God.[24] Judgments about probabilities depend greatly on moral temperament. 'In the judgment of a rightly disposed mind, objects are desirable and attainable which irreligious men will consider to be but fancies.'[25] We are responsible for our faith because we are responsible for our likes and dislikes, our hopes and opinions, upon which our faith depends.[26]

At this juncture of his argument Newman relies heavily on Aristotle. In the *Nicomachean Ethics* Aristotle maintains that things appear differently to each of us according to our own character. Our beliefs will therefore depend in some measure upon our possession of virtue or lack of it.[27] Aristotle spoke of prudence or *phronesis* as a certain virtue or mental habit needed to guide the mind to judge rightly in matters of conduct. Newman applied this prudential norm to the decision whether to believe on the basis of testimony or signs. In the *Grammar of Assent*, he coined the term 'illative sense' to describe the capacity to appraise the force of the evidence and to identify the point at which it suffices to warrant a firm conviction. Abstract logic, he argued, will never tell you when you have a sufficient accumulation of probabilities to exclude the risk of error. The farmer who is weather-wise can accurately predict when the rain will fall but will probably be unable to assign logical grounds for the prediction. The lover can tell at a glance whether the beloved is troubled or ill. In judgments of this character we rely upon a spontaneous impression in which we synthesize ingredients too varied and too subtle for enumeration.[28]

Subjective and objective factors

Comparing Newman with the evidentialists, we may say that he is engaging in what philosophers today call a 'turn to the subject.' Whereas the evidentialists emphasized the objective data, Newman is mainly concerned with the knowing subject. He rejects the idea that all minds should be bound to follow some prescribed method, as occurs in a legal proceeding. 'Rules of court,' he writes, 'are dictated by what is expedient on the whole and in the long run; but they incur the risk of being unjust to the claims of particular cases. Why am I to begin with taking up a position not my own, and unclothing my mind of that large outfit of existing thoughts, principles, likings, desires, and hopes, which make me what I am?' These personal and individual factors make up what Newman calls 'antecedent probabilities' or a priori grounds that lie at the heart of his theory of religious assent. In the *Grammar* he declares:

> It is difficult to put a limit to the legitimate force of this antecedent probability. Some minds will feel it to be so powerful, as to recognize in it almost a proof, without direct evidence, of the divinity of a religion claiming to be true, supposing its history and doctrine are free from positive objection, and there be no rival religion with plausible claims of its own.[29]

Newman, however, does not simply substitute the subject for the object. He denies only that proof must 'take a methodical form or be complete and symmetrical, in the believing mind.' Probability, he holds, is its life. Antecedent probability is what gives meaning and force to those arguments that are commonly called evidences of revelation. 'Whereas mere [antecedent] probability proves nothing, mere facts persuade no one.' Probability is to fact as the soul to the body; mere presumptions may have no force, but mere facts have no warmth. 'A mutilated and defective evidence suffices for persuasion where the heart is alive; but dead evidences, however imperfect, can but create a dead faith.'[30]

When Newman speaks of 'probability,' he is using the term in his own special sense. Probable arguments are those that do not of themselves exclude all possibility of error, as does a deductive argument from postulates or self-evident axioms in mathematics or pure logic. Probability for Newman is not opposed to certitude. Certitude in concrete matters is normally attained by an accumulation of probabilities, the assessing of which depends on personal factors that cannot be reduced to any abstract rule. In many common situations of daily life, probabilities suffice to remove doubt. For instance, most people are incapable of strictly demonstrating that Great Britain is an island; they quite properly take the multiple convergent indications as tantamount to demonstrative proof.[31]

A multiplicity of probable arguments taken together, according to Newman, can generate a firm conclusion. In one of his letters he uses the analogy of a cable made up of many strands, 'each feeble, yet together as sufficient as an iron rod.'[32] Regarding religious convictions, Newman quotes from Joseph Butler: 'Probable proofs, by being added, not only increase the evidence, but multiply it. ... The truth of our religion, like the truth of common matters, is to be judged by all the evidence taken together.'[33] The convergence of many probabilities all pointing in the same direction is itself a fact to be explained.

Assent in religious matters generally comes about through a process of informal reasoning in which the mind works spontaneously and unreflectively. It synthesizes the data with the help of antecedent probabilities. In his *Grammar of Assent* Newman gives the following description of the mental process:

> It is plain that formal logical sequence is not in fact the method by which we are enabled to become certain of what is concrete; and it is equally plain, from what has been already suggested, what the real and necessary method is. It is the cumulation of probabilities, independent of each other, arising out of the nature and circumstances of the particular case which is under review; probabilities too fine to avail separately, too subtle and circuitous to be convertible into syllogisms, too numerous and various for such conversion, even were they convertible.[34]

Newman differs from the evidentialists, therefore, not in ignoring the external evidence but in insisting on the importance of the moral and religious dispositions with which we interpret the data. In an eloquent passage from the *Grammar of Assent* he emphasizes the need for reverence:

> Many are too well inclined to sit at home, instead of stirring themselves to inquire whether a revelation has been given; they expect its evidences to come to them without their trouble; they act, not as suppliants, but as judges. Modes of argument such as Paley's, encourage this state of mind; they allow men to forget that revelation is a boon, not a debt on the part of the Giver; they treat it as a mere historical phenomenon. If I were told that some great man, a foreigner, whom I did not know, had come into town, and was on his way to call on me, and to go over [to] my house, I should send to ascertain the fact, and meanwhile I should do my best to put my house into a condition to receive him. He would not be pleased if I left the matter to take its chance, and went on the maxim that seeing was believing. Like this is the conduct of those who resolve to treat the Almighty with dispassionateness, a judicial temper, clearheadedness, and candour.[35]

The role of grace

In a number of passages Newman makes the further point that the journey to faith requires dispositions exceeding what our fallen nature can achieve by its own powers. Human nature in its present condition has lost its taste for the things of God. 'The natural man has no heart for the promises of the gospel, and dissects the evidence without reverence.'[36] But since God cannot be approached without reverence, grace is essential for the attainment of faith. 'Love of the great Object of Faith, watchful attention to Him, readiness to believe Him near, easiness to believe Him interposing in human affairs, fear of the risk of slighting or missing what may really come from Him; these are feelings not natural to fallen man, and they come only of supernatural grace.'[37] It is grace that prepares and purifies the heart so that we may perceive the things of God. It produces in us a mysterious affinity with Christ the teacher, enabling us to follow him, as it were, by instinct. Newman frequently quotes from John 10:14: 'I am the good Shepherd, and know My sheep, and am known of Mine.' And from John 10:4: 'He goeth before them, and the sheep follow Him, for they know his voice.'[38]

An instinctive leaning toward the truth of the gospel makes it possible for us to discern the presence of God in past history and present occurrences. This inclination, Newman contends, depends upon the grace of Christ, who calls his own. Grace makes it possible for the 'illative sense' to function properly in matters of religion. As Newman puts it in one of his sermons, 'The act of the mind by which an unlearned person simply believes the gospel, on the word of his teacher, may be analogous to the exercise of sagacity in a great statesman or general, supernatural grace doing for the uncultivated reason what genius does for them.'[39]

The priest who converses with Charles Reding in *Loss and Gain* apparently speaks for Newman when he tells Charles that before conversion it is possible to attain a moral certainty about the truth of the Catholic faith; that is to say, a conviction without rival conviction or reasonable doubt, but he cannot yet attain a full certitude, banishing every doubt.

> Certainty, in its highest sense, is the reward of those who, by an act of will, and at the dictate of reason and prudence, embrace the truth, when nature, like a coward, shrinks. You must make a venture; faith is a venture before a man is a Catholic; it is a gift after it. You approach the Church in the way of reason, you enter it in the light of the Spirit.[40]

Although this text seems to suggest that grace intervenes only at the moment of decision, other texts cited above make it clear that Newman was aware of the workings of grace before the actual moment of conversion. Unlike many Scholastic theologians of modern times, Newman did not concern himself with trying to apportion the roles of nature and grace in the approach to faith. What reason might be able to achieve in the absence of grace was a theoretical question that seems to have interested him very little.

A few decades later the French Jesuit Pierre Rousselot would advance the thesis that the external signs that point to the truth of the Christian religion could not give rise to a firm judgment of credibility unless they were synthesized with the help of grace, which bestows a certain connaturality with the divine. Rousselot cites in his favor an earlier passage from *Loss and Gain* where Reding and Carlton disagree on their reading of the evidence because they proceed on the basis of different unspoken presuppositions.[41] Rousselot, going beyond Newman, maintains that the infused light of faith gives the mind a 'supernatural formal object' that enables it to perceive the signs as belonging to the order of grace and revelation. Newman, although he steers clear of the technical Scholastic questions that interested Rousselot, would agree that in the concrete order of fallen human nature, the inquirer cannot arrive at true conversion without the help of grace, which illuminates the force of the evidences and makes faith possible.

Newman and post-critical personalism

Considered as a general system, Newman's epistemology certainly has its limitations. With his deep immersion in the British empiricist tradition, from Francis Bacon to David Hume, he found it hard to appreciate the capacity of the human mind to reason rigorously about matters transcending the factual and the empirical. Inclined toward nominalism, he was skeptical about universal propositions and deductive argument.[42] But even if he erred in this respect, he made a major advance in religious epistemology that could scarcely have been achieved in Scholastic circles.

In his own day Newman felt called upon to combat the myth of an autonomous realm in which reason, operating without presumptions, would deliver uncontestable conclusions. He showed that in concrete matters reason always depends on presumptions, and that these presumptions are by no means self-evident. Many of our presumptions are unconscious and merely implicit.

Since the dawn of rationalism in the seventeenth century, it had become common to hold that reason and faith were alternate routes to truth. The Deists contracted the realm of faith in order to exalt the powers of reason. At the end of the eighteenth century, Kant, reacting against the exorbitant claims of rationalism, felt obliged to narrow the range of reason in order to make room for faith. For Kant, as for the Deists, every advance of reason was seen as a defeat for faith, and every assertion of supremacy for faith was understood as a humiliation of reason.

Newman, while he might have accepted this dichotomy in his early years as an Evangelical, came to believe that faith heals reason and enables it to come fully into its own. To exclude revelation and redemption from one's consideration is not to liberate reason but to constrict it. The native dynamism of our rational nature is assisted and perfected by the solicitations of grace.

In the present age the pendulum of popular thinking has swung from objectivism to subjectivism. Few Christians have enough confidence in reason to construct systematic demonstrations of the truth of their faith. Many are quite content, as Newman and Rousselot would never have been, to say that they believe on an inner impulse, without firm rational grounds. Newman, because of his almost scrupulous concern for objective truth, would be as critical of twentieth-century subjectivism as he was of eighteenth-century evidentialism. He would, I suppose, heartily approve of the defense of philosophical reason in John Paul II's encyclical, *Faith and Reason*, which declares: 'It is faith which stirs reason to move beyond all isolation and willingly run risks so that it may attain whatever is beautiful, good, and true. Faith thus becomes the convinced and convincing advocate of reason' (§56).

Newman was quite conscious that his positions seemed to invite a kind of subjectivism or relativism with regard to truth. How does one validate one's own assumptions, if these are frequently unconscious and in any case not demonstrably true? All of us, he replied, must rely upon our own presumptions, while striving to make use of all the aids given to us. In the area of Christian evidences, he declared, 'egotism is true modesty.' And he continued:

> In religious inquiry each of us can speak only for himself, and for himself he has a right to speak. His own experiences are enough for himself, but he cannot speak for others: he cannot lay down the law; he can only bring his own experiences to the common stock of psychological facts. He knows what has satisfied and satisfies himself; if it satisfies him, it is likely to satisfy others; if, as he believes and is sure, it is true, it will approve itself to others also, for there is but one truth.[43]

Newman's views on faith and reason and his critique of evidentialism have in fact commended themselves to others. Bernard Lonergan relied heavily on Newman in developing his critique of naive realism. Newman's personalism has appealed to many post-critical thinkers of the twentieth century. The great philosopher of science, Michael Polanyi, made much of tacit awareness in drawing up what he called a 'fiduciary program.' As he was aware, his epistemology at many points resembled that of Newman.[44] Polanyi, however, was not a theologian. Newman remains the outstanding master of personalism in theological epistemology. His reflections on faith and reason have proved prophetic.

Notes

1   Newman, *Apologia pro Vita Sua* (London: Longmans, Green & Co., 1929), p. 14.

2   Newman, 'The Usurpations of Reason,' in *Fifteen Sermons Preached before the University of Oxford 1826–1843* (3rd edn, 1871, reprinted London: SPCK, n.d.), Sermon IV, pp. 54–74 at p. 58, hereafter abbreviated *OUS*.

3   'Faith and Reason Contrasted as Habits of Mind,' *OUS*, Sermon X, pp. 176–201, at p. 183.

4   Ibid., p. 185.

5   'The Nature of Faith in Relation to Reason,' *OUS*, Sermon XI, pp. 202–21, at pp. 219–20.

6   'Love the Safeguard of Faith against Superstition,' *OUS*, Sermon XII, pp. 222-50, at p. 223.

7   Ibid., p. 229.

8   Ibid., p. 239.

9   Newman, *Essays Critical and Historical*, 2 vols. (London: Longmans, Green & Co., 1895), vol. 1, pp. 30–101.

10 Quoted in Newman, *An Essay in Aid of a Grammar of Assent* (London: Longmans, Green & Co. 1901), p. 94; hereafter abbreviated *GA*.

11 'Faith and Reason Contrasted,' *OUS*, Sermon X, p. 180.

12 JHN to William R. Brownlow, 29 April 1871, *The Letters and Diaries of John Henry Newman*, 31 vols. (London: Nelson, 1961–72 Oxford: Clarendon, 1977–), vol. 25, p. 324; hereafter abbreviated *LD*.

13 John Locke, *Essay Concerning Human Understanding*, IV.19.1.

14 Ibid., IV.19.14.

15 'Love the Safeguard of Faith,' *OUS*, Sermon XII, p. 231.

16 Newman, *Essay on Development of Christian Doctrine* (Notre Dame, IN: University of Notre Dame Press, 1989), p. 328.

17 Ibid., pp. 330–1, quoting from Augustine, *De utilitate credendi*.

18 'Faith and Reason Contrasted,' *OUS*, Sermon X, p. 197.

19 *GA*, p. 425.

20 Ibid.

21 'Faith and Reason Contrasted,' *OUS*, Sermon X, p. 187.

22 'Love the Safeguard,' *OUS*, Sermon X, p. 230.

23 Ibid., p. 232.

24 Ibid., p. 241.

25   'Faith and Reason Contrasted,' *OUS*, Sermon X, p. 191.

26   Ibid., p. 192.

27   Ibid., pp. 191–2.

28   Cf. *GA*, p. 492.

29   Ibid., p. 423.

30   'Faith and Reason Contrasted,' *OUS*, Sermon X, p. 200.

31   *GA*, p. 318. Cf. Newman, *Theological Papers on Faith and Certainty* (Oxford: Clarendon, 1976), p. 19.

32   JHN to John Canon Walker, 6 July 1864, *LD*, vol. 21, p. 146.

33   *GA*, p. 319; cf. Joseph Butler, *Analogy of Religion* (New York: Ungar, 1961), pp. 238–9.

34   *GA*, p. 288.

35   Ibid., pp. 425–6.

36   'Faith and Reason Contrasted,' *OUS*, Sermon X, p. 193.

37   Ibid.

38   Ibid., p. 198.

39   'The Nature of Faith in Relation to Reason,' *OUS*, Sermon XI, p. 218.

40   Newman, *Loss and Gain: The Story of a Convert* (London: Longmans, Green & Co., 1896), pp. 384-5.

41   Pierre Rousselot, *The Eyes of Faith* (French original, 1910; English translation, New York: Fordham University Press, 1990), p. 29 refers to Newman's *Loss and Gain*, p. 364.

42   Newman's nominalism is noted by Anthony Kenny in his 'Newman as a Philosopher of Religion,' in David Brown, (ed.), *Newman, a Man for Our Time* (Harrisburg, PA: Morehouse Publishing, 1990), pp. 98–122, especially p. 100.

43   *GA*, pp. 384–5.

44   For a comparison between the two authors, see Martin X. Moleski, *Personal Catholicism: An Analysis of the Theological Epistemologies of John Henry Newman and Michael Polanyi* (Washington, DC: The Catholic University of America Press, 2000). So far as I am aware, Polanyi does not quote Newman in his published work, but he did copy out a number of passages from the *Grammar of Assent* on the indefeasibly personal character of certitude. These notes are in the Polanyi Archives at the University of Chicago, Box 24, Folder 10. I am indebted to Father Moleski for this reference.

4

The proof of Christianity

It would have been foreign to Newman's mind to write a systematic work of apologetics like the manuals of 'Christian evidences' that were in common use in his day. Deeming it impossible to bring about conversion by sheer argument, Newman distanced himself not only from Paley but also from the Roman apologists, including no doubt Giovanni Perrone, the Jesuit with whom he discussed the issues of faith and doctrinal development in 1847. Newman's sentiments are indicated in a letter to John Moore Capes of December 8, 1849:

> 'The proof of Christianity' is just the point on which polemics and dogmatics meet as on common ground. It is in the province of both, and I cannot altogether stand the Italian treatment of it, unless I mistake their words and they mine. They know nothing at all of heretics as realities – they live, at least in Rome, in a place whose boast is that it has never given birth to heresy, and they think that proofs ought to be convincing which in fact are not. Hence they are accustomed to speak of the argument for Catholicism as a demonstration, and to see no force in objections to it and admit no perplexity of intellect which is not directly and immediately wilful. This at least is their tendency in *fact*, even if I overstate their theory.[1]

Newman, however, did not reject all proofs of Christianity. Because he held that faith was in accord with reason, and was in some sense an act of reason, he was concerned to show how the act of faith could be a prudent one. Thus in *Loss and Gain* he puts on the lips of Charles Reding, the future convert, the words: 'Surely God wills us to be guided by reason; I don't mean that reason is everything, but it is at least something. Surely we ought not to act without it, against it.'[2] Newman felt the need to articulate the grounds of his own faith and to respond to the difficulties of unbelievers, such as his brother Charles and his friend William Froude, the brother of Hurrell Froude. In various writings, and especially in the *Grammar of Assent*, he lays down the elements of a treatise on apologetics, including the existence of God, the possibility of revelation, and the signs in history that revelation has in fact been given.

The existence of God

Although Newman had great admiration for Aristotle, and on many points followed him, his worldview was shaped less by Greek philosophy than by the British empirical tradition. Immersed from his youth in the works of Locke and Hume, he envisaged reality as concrete and particular. All knowledge, he believed, began with sense impressions. Any further information about essences, causes, and properties could only be a matter of inference.

What was truly foundational, for him, was an impression in one's own consciousness. Coining a variation on the famous *cogito* of Descartes, he grounded his certainty of his own existence not so much in thought as in feeling: 'Sentio ergo sum.'[3] In sensing, he held, I am borne to recognize my own existence as the sentient subject.

While never doubting that sense impressions came from external objects, Newman considered it logically possible that what we call the outside world might be an illusion. He denied that we can directly experience the external world or demonstrate its existence beyond all possible doubt. An instinct of nature drives us to believe in that world, and we have no reason for distrusting or resisting the instinct.[4]

As a boy Newman already rested in 'the thought of two and only two absolute and luminously self-evident beings, myself and my Creator.'[5] Among his earliest recollections he recorded: 'I thought life might be a dream, or I an Angel, and all this world a deception, my fellow-angels by a playful device concealing themselves from me, and deceiving me with the semblance of a material world.'[6] As an adult under the influence of Joseph Butler he would arrive at the conviction that 'material phenomena are both the types and the instruments of things unseen.'[7] Noting that this view had a certain resemblance with the idealism of Berkeley, Newman remarks that he knew little of Berkeley at that time except by name, 'nor have I ever studied him.'[8]

Apart from the self, only one other reality was to Newman absolutely certain. This other reality was God, whose voice resounds in the testimony of conscience. All normal persons, Newman believed, have a conscience that commands them categorically to do what is right and avoid what is evil. Conscience refers us to a sanction higher than the self and implies the existence of One to whom we are responsible, and before whom we stand guilty and ashamed when we have acted against its bidding. Conscience therefore impresses on the imagination the idea of a sovereign lawgiver and judge, a supreme authority whom we must obey and to whom we must render an account of our behavior.[9] It discloses God as a personal being, all-knowing, all-powerful, and all-just. Newman puts something of his argument from conscience on the lips of the fictional Callista:

> I feel that God within my heart. I feel myself in His Presence. He says to me, Do this, don't do that. You may tell me that this dictate is a mere law of my nature, as is to joy or to grieve. I cannot understand this. No, it is the echo of a person speaking to me. Nothing shall persuade me that it does not ultimately proceed from a person external to me. It carries with it its proof of its divine origin. My nature feels toward it as towards a person. When I obey it, I feel a satisfaction; when I disobey, a soreness – just like that which I feel in pleasing or offending some revered friend. ... The echo implies a voice; a voice a speaker. That speaker I love and I fear.[10]

Newman does not deny the validity of explicit proofs of the existence of God from causality and from order in the universe, but he does not rely on such proofs for his personal religion.[11] At best, he believes, such proofs can yield notional assent – an abstract affirmation that goes out not so much to the reality known as to the deliverances of our own mind. Conscience, on the contrary, confronts us directly with God as a reality to whom we are subject and upon whom we depend.

In his *Idea of a University* Newman expresses his distaste for the kind of natural theology purveyed by apologists such as Paley, who used the famous analogy of the watch and the watchmaker. Newman dismisses the argument from design on the ground that it leads at best to a powerful and wise designer who, like the God of deism, lets the machine of the universe run on by itself without any direction or interference from above. Like Hume, Newman holds that the kind of 'physical theology' represented by Samuel Clarke, far from establishing the existence of the God in whom Christians believe, only suggests some kind of supramundane finite agency analogous to the human. The God of physical theology, Newman concludes, is not very different from the God of pantheism.[12]

The need for revelation

Awareness of the self and of its God could suffice for a certain kind of natural religion, but for Newman natural religion as it actually exists contains a third ingredient, that of human need. Looking into ourselves, we are conscious of our weakness, our repeated failures, and our inability to make adequate amends. Looking about us, we find a world in which disorder prevails. The world ought to reflect the perfection of its Maker, but it does not. 'The sight of the world,' he remarks, 'is nothing else than the prophet's scroll, full of 'lamentations, mourning, and woe.''[13] The vision of the whole human race, 'having no hope and without God in the world,' is for Newman an unmistakable sign that the entire human race is implicated in some primeval catastrophe. 'Thus the doctrine of what is theologically called original sin becomes to me almost as certain as that the world exists, and as the existence of God.'[14]

It is not surprising, therefore, that natural religion, as we find it in actual practice, tends to emphasize the dark aspects of religion – a fact noted by Lucretius. Oppressed with the prevalence of sin, this religion depicts humanity as being in a degraded, servile condition and as requiring expiation in order to be reconciled with God. From the earliest books of Scripture and from the testimonies of Greek and Latin writers about the barbarous nations with which they were acquainted, Newman concludes that the practice of atonement holds a central position in natural religion.[15] Human beings are thought to be bound to one another in a solidarity of sin and reparation. Persons who are pure and holy are envisaged as sources of blessing for others who rely on their intercession.

Among the further common features of natural religion, as we find it in all times and places, Newman mentions the hope of deliverance from present suffering, confidence in divine providence, and the practices of prayer and sacrifice. People turn to God in hope that he will come to their aid, redeeming them from their extreme need and enlightening their darkness. They offer sacrifices, consecrating costly and unblemished gifts to God as means of atonement.

In view of the gravity of our need and the goodness and power of God, Newman judges it antecedently probable that God will intervene to remedy the human situation and grant a redemptive revelation in answer to the prayers and sacrifices confidently offered up to him. The hope of a message of grace and salvation is for Newman an integral part of natural religion. As is evident from what has already been said, Newman understands natural religion not in opposition to supernatural religion but in opposition to civilized or artificial religion and to religion based on the special revelation that culminates in Jesus Christ. Natural religion as he conceives of it is shot through with elements of grace. In a sermon of 1830 he expressed optimism on this score:

> The heathen ... we have reason to trust, are not in danger of perishing, except so far as all are in such danger, whether in heathen or Christian countries, leading them on by faith to their true though unseen good. For the prerogative of Christians consists in the possession, not of exclusive knowledge and spiritual aid, but of gifts high and peculiar; and though the manifestation of the Divine character in the Incarnation is a singular and inestimable benefit, yet its absence is supplied in a degree, not only in the inspired record of Moses, but even, with more or less strength, in those various traditions concerning Divine Providences and Dispensations which are scattered through the pagan mythologies.[16]

In his *The Arians of the Fourth Century* Newman presents with approval what he calls the Alexandrian doctrine of 'the divinity of traditionary religion.' With lengthy quotations from Clement of Alexandria, he maintains that 'there never was a time when God has not spoken to man,' beginning with Noah, that common father of all. God never left himself without witness in the world, and indeed in every nation. Properly speaking, therefore, revelation is a universal, not a local, gift. But natural religion is not to be confused with biblical religion, which alone is altogether true, possesses the word of God consigned to authoritative documents, celebrates the sacraments, and is attested by 'the discriminating evidence of miracles.'[17] Convinced as he is of the unique privileges of Christianity, Newman as an apologist has to consider the criteria by which it is to be recognized as revelation.

In his *Grammar of Assent* Newman takes care to differentiate his approach from that of William Paley. Paley, he says, does not require that the antecedent probability or desirability of revelation needs to be taken into account. 'He has such confidence in the strength of the testimony which he can produce in favour of the Christian miracles, that he only asks to be allowed to bring it into court.'[18] Newman too makes use of miracles and prophecies, but he warns that they are not strictly probative unless they are approached by persons whose minds are properly prepared for Christian revelation. The inquirer must be antecedently imbued with the religious opinions and sentiments that Newman has identified with natural religion.

Miracles

In the standard manuals of the day, physical miracles were strongly emphasized as the signs by which an alleged revelation could be verified. Concerned as he was with the rational grounding of faith, Newman had a lifelong interest in miracles. One of his earliest publications, written in 1825, was an encyclopedia article on biblical miracles. In 1843, when publishing a partial translation of Fleury's *Ecclesiastical History*, he composed a lengthy 'Essay on the Miracles Recorded in the Ecclesiastical History of the Early Ages.' He republished the two essays in 1870 as a 400-page volume, *Two Essays on Biblical and Ecclesiastical Miracles.*

The first essay is the more philosophical of the two. It begins with a consideration of the nature of miracles. They do not have to be violations of the laws of nature, Newman contends. An event is a miracle if it is exceptional in the order of nature but intelligible as part of a redemptive economy. From this perspective, Newman meets the objection of David Hume that it is always more likely that the testimony be false than that the account of the miracle be true. Newman would concede this if a miracle were a mere anomaly. But he contends that the biblical miracles constitute a coherent system that shows them to be parts of a higher dispensation. In view of our experience of God's beneficent providence, which Newman regards as an ingredient of natural religion, miracles may be regarded as antecedently probable.[19] The evidence for miracles is cumulative, with the probability of each being supported by that of the others.[20]

The miracles of Scripture are not random events; they support the revelation given through divine emissaries.[21] The miracle stories, moreover, are inseparably intertwined with the rest of the narrative, including the discourses of Jesus, the prophets, and the apostles.[22] It would be inconsistent, therefore, to deny the miracles while affirming the moral and religious teaching of the Bible.

It is remarkable that in his essay on biblical miracles Newman makes no special mention of Christ's resurrection, which is considered by many apologists to be the quintessential miracle that puts the divine seal on the gospel. Although Newman unquestionably considers the Resurrection as a central datum of Christian faith and hope, he does not emphasize its evidential value. In one of his finest *Parochial and Plain Sermons* he explains that Jesus refrained from showing himself to all in his glory, because the multitude would not have rightly understood or believed it. He appeared to a chosen few whose thought of him was already the mainspring of their lives. They alone were qualified to become his witnesses.[23]

In his second essay, Newman takes up ecclesiastical miracles of post-biblical times, which in the first essay he had found tainted by superstition and corruption. Correcting this unduly negative assessment, he now contends that since biblical miracles had occurred, it was antecedently likely that miracles should also take place in Church history.[24] Their occurrence would fulfill the prediction about the miraculous powers of believers at the end of Mark's Gospel.[25]

In many respects, Newman says, the two sets of miracles – biblical and ecclesiastical – resemble each other. In each case healings, exorcisms, and heavenly visions are prominent. Yet certain differences remain. For example, the ecclesiastical miracles are rarely wrought by missionaries to vindicate their own authority; they are more often worked to attest the holiness of the deceased at their tombs or through their relics.[26] The scriptural miracles occurred in forms appropriate for persuading their witnesses to adopt a religion not yet received; the ecclesiastical, for nurturing devotion among believers. It is difficult, Newman admits, to distinguish between fact and legend in the miraculous tales handed down from the early centuries of the Church. In the last chapter of his book Newman examines some particular cases, such as the 'thundering legion' that brought rain to the troops of Marcus Aurelius, the appearance of the Cross to Constantine and his army, and the discovery of the true Cross by St. Helena. Some scholars have faulted Newman for being over-credulous in his evaluations.[27]

Rather uncharacteristic of Newman the cautious inquirer, is the defiant proclamation of credulity in his *The Present Position of Catholics in England*:

> For myself, lest I appear in any way to be shrinking from a determinate judgment on the claims of some of those miracles and relics, which Protestants are so startled at, and to be hiding particular questions in what is vague and general, I will avow distinctly, that, putting out of the question the hypothesis of unknown law of nature (that is, of the professed miracle not being miraculous), I think it impossible to withstand the evidence which is brought for the liquefaction of the blood of St. Januarius at Naples, and for the motion of the eyes of the pictures of the Madonna in the Roman States. I see no reason to doubt the material of the Lombard crown at Monza; and I do not see why the Holy Coat at Trèves may not have been what it professes to be. I firmly believe that portions of the True Cross are at Rome and elsewhere, that the Crib of Bethlehem is at Rome, and the bodies of St. Peter and St. Paul also. ... I firmly believe that saints in their life-time have before now raised the dead to life, crossed the sea without vessels, multiplied grain and bread, cured incurable diseases, and superseded the operation of the laws of the universe in a multitude of ways.[28]

Anxious as Newman is to defend both biblical and ecclesiastical miracles, he is reserved about their apologetical force. While granting that miracles were in some cases convincing to those who witnessed them, later generations, he believes, cannot ascertain the credibility of the accounts unless appeal be made, in the case of biblical miracles, to the doctrine of inspiration – an appeal that presupposes faith.

One of the *Parochial and Plain Sermons* bears the significant title, 'Miracles No Remedy for Unbelief.'[29] In it Newman contends that the Israelites of old were not as a group much better than the generality of mankind. Evil men such as Dathan, Korah, Saul, and Joab have their parallels all over the world. The sight of miracles does not make people believe and obey, nor is the absence of miracles an excuse for not believing and obeying. 'If they do not hear Moses and the prophets,' says Jesus, 'neither will they be convinced' if some one should rise from the dead' (Lk. 16:31).

While it is extremely improbable that Christianity could have been established without miracles, we do not today believe primarily on account of the miracles. Christianity, Newman contends, has other marks of its truth such as prophecy, the disclosure of sublime truths, the exemplary character of Jesus Christ, the 'notes' of the Church, and the purity of Christian moral teaching.[30]

Prophecy

In his *Essays on Miracles* Newman restricts his treatment to physical miracles, which he describes as 'the most striking and conclusive evidence' in favor of the Jewish and Christian revelations.[31] In his *Grammar of Assent*, however, he deals at greater length with prophecy. He explains at considerable length that Jesus was the Messiah predicted in the Old Testament – the man born of the tribe of Judah, in whom all the tribes of the earth were to be blessed. He points to many texts in the New Testament in which the authors depict the history of Jesus as an accomplishment of prophecy. Jesus himself not infrequently appeals to Old Testament prophecies in evidence of his own divine mission, while uttering new prophecies in his own name.

Newman admits that prophecies, being figurative, vague, and ambiguous, are often difficult to interpret except in the light of their fulfillment. Only from the gospel history can we understand how the Messiah could both suffer and be victorious; how his kingdom would be inherited by the true children of Abraham and yet be open to the Gentiles. It is not surprising, therefore, that the Jews before the time of Christ were confused about the promises in their own Scriptures and partly for that reason failed to recognize the Messiah when he came. We today still experience difficulty in making sense of the eschatological texts in the Book of Revelation. Jesus, according to Newman, transfigured the old prophecies and brought to light the mystery hidden in them.

Historical argument

In the last chapter of the *Grammar of Assent* Newman spells out the kind of objective evidence that he finds supportive of Christian faith. Instead of relying as Paley does on miracles, he points to what he calls coincidences – events which, 'though not in themselves miraculous, do irresistibly force upon us, almost by the law of our nature, the presence and extraordinary action of Him whose being we already acknowledge.'[32] An example might be the reception of a greatly needed and unexpected gift soon after the prayer of a saintly person.

In a global survey of world history, Newman contemplates the wonder of Jewish monotheism that persisted for two thousand years amid the polytheistic religions of the surrounding peoples. He portrays Jesus as having fulfilled the types and prophecies of the Old Testament and having interpreted these by the particular way in which he fulfilled them. The Divine Master, he declares, 'explains and in a certain sense corrects, the prophecies of the Old Covenant, by a more exact interpretation of them from Himself.'[33]

Newman also makes much of the fact that the Jews' rejection of Jesus as their Messiah was catastrophic for the nation. 'They fell under the power of their enemies, and were overthrown, their holy city razed to the ground, their polity destroyed, and the remnant of their people cast off to wander far and away through every land except their own, as we find them to this day.'[34] This reversal of fortunes, Newman speculates, must have a meaning if there is a God.

As a patristic scholar, Newman shows particular interest in the conversion of the Roman Empire. According to our Lord's announcement, he says, Christianity was to prevail and become a great empire; but it was to accomplish this destiny not by force of arms or other worldly means but by 'the novel expedient of sanctity and suffering.'[35] Only divine power can adequately explain how this remarkable success was achieved by means that seemed so unsuited to the purpose.

Can an alternative explanation be offered? Edward Gibbon, in his *The Decline and Fall of the Roman Empire*, had enumerated five causes for the success of Christianity: the zeal of Christians, their doctrine of future rewards and punishments, their claim to miracles, their sober and domestic virtues, and their efficient ecclesiastical organization. Even if these five factors did figure to some degree, Newman replies, Gibbon did not account for the presence of all of them together in one religion, nor did he explain why Christians were so zealous, virtuous, and efficient as compared with their contemporaries.

Newman also faults Gibbon for failing to show that his five factors did in fact contribute to the propagation of the Christian faith. As for zeal, Christians had it after they were converted, but it did not make them Christians. So too, the doctrine of eternal rewards and punishments would influence believing Christians but it would be ridiculed by unbelievers. The claim to miracles was rarely asserted by the Christian apologists, perhaps because the Hellenistic sects had plenty of wonder-workers of their own. The 'sober and domestic virtues,' by Gibbon's own admission, presented a 'gloomy and austere aspect,' and would have been viewed with disgust by pagans, as they were by Gibbon himself. The ecclesiastical organization developed slowly, and when it did develop, it functioned more as a stabilizing than as an expansive force. It could not account for the Church's dynamism.

Newman's personalist apologetic

In place of Gibbon's five causes, Newman proposes a single cause, the image of Christ, who 'inspired that zeal which the historian so poorly comprehends.'[36] The affections of the early Christians are focused on Christ, whom they love without seeing. Dwelling in the hearts of the faithful, he is the true principle of conversion and of fellowship among the believers. His image, as the vivifying idea of Christianity, evokes some of the phenomena noted by the historian, such as the exemplary lives of the Christians, their longing for heaven, and their invincible adherence to their faith.

In the concluding pages of his *Grammar of Assent* Newman gives a series of stirring quotations from early Christian witnesses, such as Ignatius of Antioch, Polycarp, Justin Martyr, the *Letter to Diognetus*, Tertullian, and the *Acts of the Martyrs*. He shows that the saints and martyrs were indeed driven by an intense and ecstatic love for the Crucified Savior, whom they hailed as the Bread of Life and as their Guardian, Father, Teacher, Counselor, Physician, and Friend.

Newman does not limit his argument to past events but carries it into the present. The promised Deliverer, he asserts, having passed beyond this life, still continues to exert his power through visible symbols and sacraments, as though he were still in our midst on this earth.[37] The self-perpetuation of this dynamic Image is evidence that Christ continues to fulfill the revelatory and transformative role assigned to him in Hebrew prophecy. The voice of the Good Shepherd is recognized by those whom he calls to himself.[38]

Newman's personalism, manifest in his explanation of the devotion of believers, reappears when he treats the means by which faith is transmitted. The fifth of his Oxford University Sermons, preached in 1832, is on 'Personal Influence, the Means of

Propagating the Truth.' The mission of Jesus, he says, was not simply to communicate a set of beliefs but to change the hearts of his hearers, making them like his own.[39] Jesus' evident holiness was what ignited the affection and loyalty of his intimate followers, who felt themselves individually addressed and invited by his example.[40] With the image of his personal presence in their minds, they began to be transformed into images of him, and were trained to succeed him in the propagation of the truth. Each saintly witness receives and transmits the sacred flame.[41]

In the end, therefore, Newman does not rely so much on external signs as on the inner call of grace and the fidelity with which that call is obeyed. In the previously mentioned sermon denying the power of miracles to generate belief, Newman declares that the true cause of unbelief and disobedience is the lack of love of God. 'If we do not love God,' Newman told his congregation, 'it is because we have not wished to love Him, tried to love Him, prayed to love Him.' Love of heaven is, in the end, the only way to heaven.[42]

In exalting love as the way to heaven, Newman does not make it a substitute for rational grounds. I take him to mean rather that where such love is present, sincere inquirers will be able to find sufficient evidence for at least a rudimentary faith in God. If they are privileged to encounter a religion accredited by divine signs, they will be able to recognize and embrace it. But if their hearts are hardened, the evidences will be wasted upon them.

Value of Newman's apologetics

Newman stands with Origen and Augustine, Aquinas and Pascal, as one of the great apologists of all time. He is outstanding for constructing his arguments in the light of the profound and realistic theory of religious knowledge that we have examined in the preceding chapter. In addition, he possessed a remarkable command of the biblical and patristic sources, which he effectively marshalled in his presentations. As a master of English prose, he set forth his arguments with striking eloquence.

On certain points Newman's apologetics calls for further comment. His approach to the existence of God probably under-estimates the value of the traditional philosophical proofs, which were familiar to him only in debased form, as presented in British 'physical theology.' He was by his own admission little inclined toward metaphysics. But his argument from conscience is un-questionably impressive; it compares favorably with the moral proofs for rewards and punishments in a future life proposed by Plato and Kant. Newman succeeds in finding an argument with a strong experiential basis and one that directly points to a personal God, to whom we are related as lawgiver and judge. Although Newman did not claim that his argument from conscience was a cogent proof of God's existence, it undoubtedly has great persuasive power to persons who have a keen sense of moral obligation. It is to such persons that Newman desires to speak.

Newman made a major contribution by bringing out the importance of what he called 'natural religion' as a presupposition for the effectiveness of any *demonstratio christiana*. His defense of natural religion and of its affinity with biblical and Christian faith provides a welcome alternative not only to the natural theologies of the Enlightenment but also to the revelational positivism of authors such as Karl Barth, who reject natural religion and disregard the subjective capacity of the human person to receive the word of God.

Newman's general theory of miracles stands up well under the passage of time. He corrected the popular impression that miracles are mere anomalies or arbitrary acts of divine power. They are, as he showed, integral parts of a whole supernatural dispensation in which they have coherence and meaning. He also showed that for persons who accept the truths of natural religion, miracles are antecedently probable. In this way he effectively answered the critique forcefully stated by David Hume.

Newman, moreover, did not exaggerate the probative force of miracles. In his writings on the subject he was more concerned to vindicate the reliability of Scripture and of the patristic witnesses than to show how people of modern times can be converted by reports of miracles that had occurred long in the past. He insisted only that the miracles of Christ and the apostles had been instrumental in the launching of the faith.

Newman's use of Scripture in his discussion of miracles and prophecies appears dated to the modern reader, who would expect some use to be made of tools such as source criticism, form criticism, and redaction criticism. For similar reasons Newman's assessment of individual miracle stories in early Church history stands in need of revision. His enthusiastic embrace of modern ecclesiastical miracles in his Lectures of 1851 can best be understood in the context of the triumphalistic tone of his anti-Protestant polemic.

In discussing the conversion of the Roman Empire, Newman shows his consummate mastery of the patristic texts. One must admit, however, that massive historical movements of this kind do not easily lend themselves to a single clear interpretation. A vast number of economic, social, and cultural factors were at work. Without faulting his analysis, the contemporary reader will no doubt wish to supplement it with more recent sociological approaches.[43]

Finally, Newman's treatment of personal witness is a refreshing innovation, supplying for a deficiency in the standard apologetical literature of the day. The testimony of convinced believers has a spontaneous persuasive power exceeding that of complex rational proofs. Perpetuating the tradition of Newman, twentieth-century authors such as Gabriel Marcel and Maurice Nédoncelle have effectively used his personalist conception of testimony in their philosophy of religion.

Notes

1   *The Letters and Diaries of John Henry Newman*, 31 vols. (London: Nelson, 1961–72 Oxford: Clarendon, 1977–), vol. 13, pp. 333–4; hereafter abbreviated *LD*.

2   Newman, *Loss and Gain: The Story of a Convert* (London: Longmans, Green & Co., 1896), p. 110.

3   From a manuscript of 1859 excerpted by James Collins in his *Philosophical Readings in Cardinal Newman* (Chicago: Regnery, 1961), pp. 193–4.

4   Newman, *An Essay in Aid of a Grammar of Assent* (London: Longmans, Green & Co., 1901), p. 62; hereafter abbreviated *GA*. In the summer of 1869, Newman submitted the galleys of this work to the Rev. Dr. Charles Meynell, who taught philosophy at Oscott Seminary. In letters of July 25 and August 17 to Meynell, Newman defended his view that 'belief in an external world is an instinct on the apprehension of sensible phenomena;' he also explained in what sense he was using the word 'instinct.' See Collins, *Philosophical Readings*, pp. 197–201.

5   Newman, *Apologia pro Vita Sua* (London: Longmans, Green & Co, 1929), p. 4; hereafter *Apol*.

6   Ibid., p. 2.

7   Ibid., p. 18.

8   Ibid.

9   *GA*, pp. 103–15. Cf. Newman, 'Letter to the Duke of Norfolk,' *Certain Difficulties Felt by Anglicans in Catholic Teaching*, 2 vols. (London: Longmans, Green & Co., 1910), vol. 2, pp. 246–61; hereafter abbreviated *Diff*. In his *Philosophical Notebook* Newman penned between 1859 and 1868 a

text entitled 'Proof of Theism' in which he explains that the sense of moral obligation carries with it the notion of future judgment and thus of a Judge or Recompensor. See *The Philosophical Notebook of John Henry Newman*, 2 vols., ed. E. A. Sillem and rev. by A. J. Boekraad (Louvain: Nauwelaerts, 1970), vol. 2, pp. 31–61, especially pp. 59–60.

10   Newman, *Callista* (London: Longmans, Green & Co., 1881), pp. 314–15.

11   *Apol.*, p. 241.

12   Newman, *The Idea of a University Defined and Illustrated* (London: Longmans, Green & Co., 1896), p. 454.

13   *Apol.*, p. 241.

14   Ibid., pp. 242–3.

15   *GA*, pp. 292–3.

16   'The Influence of Natural and Revealed Religion Respectively,' Sermon II of *Fifteen Sermons Preached Before the University of Oxford* (London: SPCK, n.d., reprinted from 3rd edn, 1871), pp. 16–36, at p. 33; hereafter abbreviated *OUS*.

17   Newman, *The Arians of the Fourth Century*, 3rd edn (London: Longmans, Green & Co., 1871; reprint 1897), pp. 79–89; hereafter abbreviated *Miracles*.

18   *Apol.*, p. 329.

19   Newman, *Two Essays on Biblical and Ecclesiastical Miracles* (London: Longmans, Green & Co., 1907), p. 20.

20   Ibid., p. 8.

21   Ibid., p. 23.

22   Ibid., p. 36.

23   'Witnesses of the Resurrection,' *Parochial and Plain Sermons*, one-volume edition (San Francisco: Ignatius, 1987), 1:21, pp. 179–86; hereafter abbreviated *PPS*.

24   *Miracles*, p. 103.

25   Ibid., pp. 113–14, 192.

26   Ibid., p. 220–1.

27   Stanley L. Jaki mentions in this connection the critiques written by T. H. Huxley, E. A. Abbott, and André Bremond. See his *Newman's Challenge* (Grand Rapids, MI: Eerdmans, 2000), pp. 60–2.

28   Newman, *Lectures on the Present Position of Catholics in England* (London: Longmans, Green & Co., 1896), pp. 312–13.

29   *PPS*, vol. 8, p. 6, pp. 1599–1606.

30   Ibid., p. 94. In a letter to Baron Emly of April 17, 1883, Newman declared that for the past fifty years he had believed that miracles were a proof of the divinity of Christianity only at the time of its coming. A contemporary

Christian apologist should use other arguments such as the wonderful properties of the Church. The arguments must always be personal and cumulative. See *LD* vol. 30, pp. 206–7.

31   *Miracles*, p. 7.

32   *GA*, p. 427.

33   Ibid., p. 454.

34   Ibid., p. 434.

35   Ibid., p. 456.

36   Ibid., p. 465.

37   Ibid., p. 489.

38   Ibid., p. 492.

39   'Personal Influence, the Means of Propagating the Truth,' *OUS*, Sermon V, pp. 75–98, at p. 87.

40   Ibid., p. 95.

41   Ibid., p. 97.

42   *PPS*, 8:6, pp. 1599–1606.

43   See, for example, Rodney Stark, *The Rise of Christianity: A Sociologist Reconsiders History* (Princeton, NJ: Princeton University Press, 1996).

5

Revelation, doctrine, development

Newman, as we have seen, distinguishes between natural and revealed religion. By the latter he means the special strand of religion that arose in ancient Israel and came to a culmination in Jesus Christ. This revelation, taught in Holy Scripture, 'is from God in a sense in which no other doctrine can be said to be from Him.'[1] The Israelites of old and the Christians of today have in their canonical Scriptures authoritative documents of revelation, and in their sacraments appointed channels of communication with God, that are not available to humankind in general.[2]

Scripture and tradition

Newman, like many of his contemporaries in England, was raised on what he called 'biblical religion.' Even as a boy, he recalls, he was 'brought up to take great delight in reading the Bible.'[3] From youth he accepted the sixth of the Anglican Thirty-nine Articles, which states that everything necessary for salvation is contained in the Bible or at least provable from it. But he never understood this Article as denying that tradition is a necessary help for understanding the Bible. Even as a Catholic he still found it possible to hold the sufficiency of Scripture, provided that Scripture be broadly understood as containing all that Christians can derive from it by pondering its meaning in the light of tradition. The dispute between Anglicans and Catholics about the sufficiency of Scripture, he came to believe, is mainly a matter of words. Anglicans do not hold that all revelation is in Scripture in such a way that the solitary reader can extract it by pure, unaided logic; nor do Catholics deny that every doctrine of the faith can be found in Scripture, at least in some secondary or symbolic sense.[4]

From the time of his ordination in the Church of England Newman persisted in maintaining that the Bible was not an adequate instrument for conveying the full word of God. Scripture, he declared, was written for the instruction and consolation of persons who were already believers.[5] Without the mediation of tradition we would be incapable of identifying the inspired books or assuring ourselves that the texts are not corrupt.

Most Christians, Newman observed, get their faith first of all from their parents and only later become readers of the Bible.[6] Once they have been educated in the faith with the help of the tradition and the creeds, they can find supporting evidence in the Bible. But if they go to the Bible without previous formation, they can fall into all sorts of idiosyncratic and perverse opinions. It is presumptuous, therefore, to reject all helps but reading the Bible.[7] The principle that the Bible alone can teach the word of God has been, from the beginning, the very seedbed of heresy.[8] In 1838, in his eighty-fifth *Tract for the Times*, he contends that 'those who try to form their Creed by Scripture only fall away from the Church and her doctrines, and join one or other sect or party,' because many truths taught by the Church are 'not directly stated in Scripture'[9]

Throughout his career as an ordained priest, first Anglican and then Catholic, Newman continued to pummel the doctrine that Scripture alone was a sufficient guide to faith. Many beliefs characteristic of Protestantism, he pointed out, are not clearly taught in Scripture: for instance, infant baptism and the observance of Sunday as the Lord's Day, 'to say nothing of the fundamental principle that the Bible and the Bible only is the religion of Protestants.'[10]

Ever since Edward Hawkins convinced him of the importance of tradition, Newman nourished his faith on the witness of Christian antiquity. Apostolic tradition, as he understood it, did not detract from the sovereign authority of Scripture but served, in combination with Scripture, to refute 'the self-authorized, arbitrary doctrines of the heretics.'[11] The Fathers, for Newman, represented the mind of the whole, undivided Church. 'What was in an early age held universally, must at least in spirit have been unconsciously transmitted from the Apostles, if there is no reason against it, and must be the expression of their mind and wishes, under changed circumstances, and therefore is binding on us in piety, even though not part of the Faith.'[12]

As an Anglican, Newman repeatedly invoked the formula of Vincent of Lerins, that we are bound to believe what has been professed by Christians 'everywhere, always, and by all.'[13] But he added the reservation that the rule could not be applied mechanically but only with practical judgment and good sense.[14] It would be impossible to make a mathematically complete survey of all the Fathers or to specify exactly what constitutes an agreement among them.

Episcopal and prophetical tradition

Newman recognized that tradition was a very broad category, containing materials of varying importance and authenticity. The core of Christian tradition, in his view, consisted of truths formally sealed and handed down as stemming from the apostles and as requiring assent. By this he apparently meant the primitive 'rule of faith,' from which the earliest creeds derived. He called this kind of tradition 'episcopal,' because he saw it as 'committed and received from Bishop to Bishop,' and as forced on the attention of individual Christians, to be received by them in the measure of their capacities.[15]

Surrounding this indispensable core was a vast and amorphous collection of ideas and customs that might in some way stem from the apostles though it had developed in varied forms, according to the diversity of places and cultures. This broader stream, Newman believed, was at some points hardly separable from episcopal tradition, but at other points it bordered on fable and legend. It was:

> partly written, partly unwritten, partly the interpretation, partly the supplement of Scripture, partly preserved in intellectual expressions, partly latent in the spirit and temper of Christians; poured to and fro in closets and upon the housetops, in liturgies, in controversial works, in obscure fragments, in sermons, in popular prejudices, in local customs.[16]

This unofficial tradition Newman called 'prophetical,' on the ground that prophets are called to expound what apostles and bishops formally teach. Prophetical tradition, he believed, was generally consonant with episcopal tradition, but could be corrupted in its details. The Church accordingly allows some freedom for her members to entertain doubts about the truth of matters contained in prophetical tradition.

In his Anglo-Catholic period Newman argued that the Catholic churches (whether Roman, Greco-Russian, or Anglican) were one in their acceptance of episcopal tradition but differed in their prophetical traditions. Later, as a Catholic, he became convinced that the differences were not confined to the realm of elective opinions but also included obligatory tenets of faith. As he came to accept a dynamically developing theory of doctrine he was able to integrate episcopal and prophetic tradition in a single stream exhibiting both continuity and change.[17]

Authority and interpretation of scripture

For all his reverence toward the Fathers, Newman was convinced that in some respects Scripture enjoyed a dignity superior to tradition. 'Scripture has a gift which Tradition has not; it is fixed, tangible, accessible, readily applicable, and besides all this is perfectly true in all its parts and relations; in a word, it is a sacred *text*.'[18] The inspired Gospels preserve the words and teachings of Jesus and reflect his manner of speaking. The rest of the New Testament does not so much increase revelation as comment upon it.[19]

In Tract 85, composed in 1838, Newman, challenging the position that a solid faith could be built on Scripture alone, piled up objections to the historical accuracy of Scripture and to the authority of the canon so forcefully that he could be accused of playing into the hands of skeptics. His purpose, however, was to demonstrate the necessity of the Church and her tradition.

As a Roman Catholic Newman continued to wrestle with the doctrines of the inspiration and inerrancy of Scripture, especially after these doctrines were formally promulgated by the First Vatican Council (1870). In one of his last articles, published in 1884, he argued that the Council could not have meant to teach that the true and inerrant meaning is the obvious sense that the unsophisticated reader would find in the text. For, as both Trent and Vatican I had declared, it was the prerogative of the Church to judge the true meaning of Scripture.[20] Surprisingly, perhaps, Newman does not follow Origen and Augustine in admitting that the historical sense may be erroneous, provided that the spiritual sense be true. Whatever Scripture sets forth in the form of historical narrative, he holds, must be true in its historical sense.[21]

Keenly aware of the difficulties being raised in his day against the scientific and historical accuracy of the Bible, Newman qualified the principle just stated by a further explanation. Inspiration, he held, is a positive assistance from the Holy Spirit giving the text a moral or religious meaning intended by God, but possibly hidden from the human author. Limited in its range, inspiration does not dispel all ignorance from the minds of the human writers. The essential is that the biblical teaching on matters of faith and moral conduct be true. This will include the substantial historicity of events connected with God's plan of redemption, but allows for inaccuracies in matters of historical detail that have no bearing on faith and morals. These inaccuracies are referable to the human element in the composition.

Newman's article was promptly attacked by a theology professor from Maynooth, the future bishop John Healy, who denied that there could be any error at all in the canonical Scriptures. Newman replied rather fiercely, especially in the original manuscript version, in which he rebuked one who 'with so little preparation' dared 'to deliver crude judgments upon a Cardinal of Holy Church.'[22] He continued to insist that Holy Scripture contains *obiter dicta* that are not binding on the faith of Christians.[23] He did not make it clear how to reconcile the inaccuracies of detail with his professed view that Scripture is inspired in all its parts.[24]

In 1893, after Newman's death, Leo XIII published the encyclical *Providentissimus Deus*, which rejected the limitation of inspiration and inerrancy to matters of faith and morals, as if inspiration were compatible with error in details of history and science. Leo could easily be understood as having condemned Newman's position. But seventy years later, Vatican II, in its Constitution on Divine Revelation, taught that the Bible was free from error in teaching 'that truth which God wanted to put into the sacred writings for the sake of our salvation.'[25] This phrasing can probably be squared with the essentials of Newman's position. While some of Newman's expressions may have been unfortunate, his thoughts on inspiration and inerrancy in many ways anticipate what has by now become the common teaching of Catholics.

In the interpretation of Scripture, Newman consistently defended the 'allegorical method' exemplified by the school of Alexandria. This method claimed some warrant in the practice of

Jesus, who taught by way of parables, adumbrating great truths by means of lesser.[26] Biblical history, Newman believed, is replete with prophecies and types whereby the earlier foreshadows that which is to come. Pursuing these higher truths, the Alexandrians sometimes fell into excesses, weakening the force of historical facts and doctrinal declarations.[27] But their principles were essentially sound.

Far more serious, in Newman's judgment, were the errors of literalist exegetes such as Theodore of Mopsuestia, the master of Nestorius. Against Theodore and the school of Antioch Newman writes, with an eye on the historical-critical exegetes of his own day:

> In all ages of the Church, her teachers have shown a disinclination to confine themselves to the mere literal interpretation of Scripture. Her most subtle and powerful method of proof, whether in ancient or modern times, is the mystical sense, which is so frequently used in doctrinal controversy as on many occasions to supersede any other. In the early centuries we find this method of interpretation to be the very ground for receiving as revealed the doctrine of the Holy Trinity. Whether we betake ourselves to the Ante-Nicene writers or the Nicene, certain texts will meet us, which do not obviously refer to that doctrine, yet are put forward as palmary proofs of it. . . . It may almost be laid down as an historical fact that the mystical interpretation and orthodoxy will stand or fall together.[28]

Newman particularly reproaches Theodore for maintaining that 'the real sense of Scripture was, not the scope of a Divine Intelligence, but the intention of the mere human organ of inspiration.'[29] These exegetical principles, Newman maintains, lead directly to the separation between the divinity and the humanity of Christ as professed by Nestorius.[30]

Revelation as impression and idea

Newman consistently taught that revelation primordially took the form of God's action in history. Unlike natural religion, revealed religion begins with facts and deeds that apprise us of the reality and the intentions of God.[31] But these facts are not revelation in the full sense until the meaning is brought home to a human mind; rather, they are instruments that impress upon the mind what God wishes it to know. Especially in his Anglican writings, Newman speaks of revelation as an 'impression' – an immediate datum of experience arising directly from contact with realities beyond us. But increasingly after 1840 he describes revelation as an 'idea.' In his *Essay on Development* he explains an idea as an active principle that takes hold of the mind and leads to ever-new contemplation of itself.[32] Christian revelation as an idea has three principal attributes: it is comprehensive, living, and real.[33]

It is *comprehensive*. 'Creeds and dogmas,' writes Newman, 'live in the one idea which they are designed to express, and which alone is substantive; and are necessary because the human mind cannot reflect upon that idea except piecemeal, cannot use it in its oneness and entireness, nor without resolving it into a series of aspects and relations.'[34] The unitary idea of Christianity underlies all its expressions, whether in doctrine, worship, or behavior. As a 'master vision,' Newman believes, the constitutive idea of Christianity 'unconsciously supplies the mind with spiritual life and peace.'[35]

Secondly, Christianity is a *living* idea. It takes hold of the minds in which it lodges. It establishes itself by entering into relations, whether friendly or hostile, with the prevalent opinions, principles, and institutions of the communities in which it dwells. It runs the risk of contamination from intercourse with human cultures, but is capable of authentically expanding through trial and error. In this connection Newman enunciates his famous maxim, 'In a higher world it is otherwise, but here below to live is to change, and to be perfect is to have changed often.'[36]

Lastly, Christianity is a *real* idea. Influenced by the Alexandrian Platonist tradition, Newman rebelled against the conception that ideas are simply mental constructs. For him, the idea pre-exists before entering the mind. 'The mind,' he writes, 'is below truth.'[37] Through the appearances of nature and the symbols of Scripture, liturgy, and dogma, God communicates mysterious and heavenly truth to which the human mind is receptive but nevertheless unequal. The Christian idea is the living impression on the human mind made by truth that, without change or alteration, communicates itself in various ways. The Church and all her mysteries and sacraments 'are but expressions in human language of truths to which the human mind is unequal.'[38]

The move to dogma

Revelation, in Newman's judgment, was essentially mysterious. 'No revelation can be complete and systematic, from the weakness of the human intellect; *so far as* it is not such, it is mysterious.'[39] As believers we submit in utter reverence to truth that remains far above our powers of comprehension. In his early book on Arianism, Newman argued that in the abstract, a religion without creedal formulas and dogmas would be the best, because 'when confessions do not exist, the mysteries of divine truth, instead of being exposed to the gaze of the profane and uninstructed, are kept hidden in the bosom of the Church, far more faithfully than is otherwise possible.'[40] But in the course of time heretics, 'insulting its [the Church's] silence,' unsettled the faithful and required the Church to render authoritative judgment on points in dispute.[41]

Terms not found in Scripture may be needed to preserve the faith at a time when heretics are distorting the meaning of Scripture. The paradigmatic instance is the definition of the 'consubstantiality' of the Son with the Father by the First Council of Nicaea. The bishops adopted the technical term 'consubstantial' (*homoousion*) to preclude the evasions of the Arian party. The Nicene dogma was not an addition to the apostolic faith but, as Athanasius put it, a summation of the sense of Scripture.[42]

As he drew closer to Rome, Newman moved beyond his merely defensive view of dogma and took a more positive view of the process of dogmatization. An important stage of the transition is marked by the last of his Oxford University Sermons, preached on the Feast of the Purification of Mary, February 2, 1843.[43] At the outset Newman notes that Holy Scripture on several occasions describes Mary as keeping what was said to her in her heart and pondering it (Lk. 2:10, 51). For her it was not enough to assent to God's word; she dwelt upon it, making use of her reason in order to penetrate its meaning and implications.

Applying this to the Church as a community, Newman maintains that the inward idea of divine truth, once communicated, passes into explicit form by the activity of human reflective powers. Religious people have a 'master view' that they seek progressively to translate into formulated truths. Thanks to the probings of their devout curiosity, they formulate mental propositions and gradually succeed in putting these into words, so that the truth they have embraced may be solidified and transmitted to others.[44] The sacred impression of divine truth upon their minds serves as a regulating principle, preventing heretical distortions. The inspired statements of Scripture provide the main outlines; they initiate but do not exhaust the process of dogmatization. The dogmatic statements of the creed do not enlarge upon the Christian idea, but only express aspects of it. Thus 'the Catholic dogmas are, after all, but symbols of a Divine fact, which, far from being compassed by those very propositions, would not be exhausted, nor fathomed, by a thousand.'[45] Eventually all doctrines run up against their limits and open out upon the divine mystery.

Importance of dogma

From the age of fifteen, Newman recalls, he always professed a dogmatic faith – one ineluctably bound up with definite propositions, such as the tripersonal being of God, the Incarnation, and other articles of the creed. Before he was sixteen, he drew up a series of biblical texts in support of each verse of the Athanasian Creed.[46] By the middle 1830s he was convinced that his primary battle was with liberalism, by which he meant 'the antidogmatic principle and its developments.'[47] In his *Essay on Development* he defines dogmas as 'supernatural truths irrevocably committed to human language, imperfect because it is human, but definitive and necessary because given from above.'[48] John and Paul and the early Fathers are consistent, Newman contends, in holding that the profession of truth has a bearing on salvation. Christ himself died as a witness to the truth – a truth that was definite, formal, and independent of believers.[49]

So engrossing was the struggle for dogma in Newman's life that, in his speech upon receiving the *biglietto* officially informing him of his appointment as cardinal, he could claim that his career had been dedicated to combating liberalism, which he described as 'the doctrine that there is no positive truth in religion' and which he prophetically characterized as 'an error overspreading, as a snare, the whole earth.'[50] Many years earlier, in the *Essay on Development*, he had taken aim at the same aberration, describing liberalism rather fully:

That truth and falsehood in religion are but matter of opinion; that one doctrine is as good as another; that the Governor of the world does not intend that we should gain the truth; that there is no truth; that we are not more acceptable to God by believing this than by believing that; that no one is answerable for his opinions; that they are a matter of necessity or accident; that it is enough if we sincerely hold what we profess; that our merit lies in seeking, not in possessing; that it is a duty to follow what seems to us true, without fear lest it should not be true; that it may be a gain to succeed, and can be no harm to fail; that we may take up and lay down opinions at pleasure, that belief belongs to the mere intellect, not to the heart also; that we may safely trust to ourselves in matters of Faith, and need no other guide, – this is the principle of philosophies and heresies, which is very weakness.[51]

More specifically, Newman opposed two schools of thought that had made great progress in England in the eighteenth century. The first was Latitudinarianism, which reduced the faith to a few basic gospel truths that were scarcely more than a republication of the law of nature.[52] The second was Evangelicalism, which promoted a religion of the heart, relegating ideas and convictions to a realm of privacy. Newman, for his part, was utterly convinced that God had imparted through revelation a definite message that was capable of satisfying and regenerating not only the feelings but also the convictions both of individuals and of societies.

Development of doctrine

In the early 1840s, Newman's problem was to discern the truth amid competing systems of dogma. As an Anglican he had maintained that the faith of the apostles came to expression in the consensus of the Fathers and in the creeds and dogmas of the patristic age. The Anglican *via media*, with its criterion of apostolicity, was a golden mean between Protestantism, which subtracted from the fullness of apostolic faith, and Roman Catholicism, which had added to it and thereby corrupted it.

At various times in his Anglo-Catholic period Newman tried to specify some of the Roman corruptions. In this category he frequently listed doctrines such as papal infallibility, transubstantiation, the Mass as a sacrifice distinct from Calvary, and Purgatory as a place of torment, as well as practices such as traffic in indulgences, the cult of relics and images, and quasi-divine honors paid to the saints and especially to the Blessed Virgin Mary. By 1841, when he wrote his Tract 90, Newman took the position that the Thirty-nine Articles, having been written before Trent, did not directly repudiate the teaching of that Council. While Newman found little to blame in the utterances of Trent, he was still convinced that the Roman church tolerated and encouraged many false teachings and superstitious practices.

As an Anglo-Catholic, Newman was faced with a battle on two

fronts. In opposition to the Protestants, he had to establish that authoritative doctrine had developed beyond the bare assertions of Holy Scripture. Since the Arians, Nestorians, Eutychians, and other heretics had considerable constituencies in the early Church, no consensus existed on trinitarian and Christological doctrine until conciliar decisions of the fourth and fifth centuries. Since these decisions had been incorporated into the Anglican formularies, the principle of dogmatic development had to be accepted by Anglicans. Against Rome, Newman had to show that the doctrines of the ancient Church were still a sufficient guide and that the developments of later councils and popes were corruptions. Only then could it be claimed that the *via media* was sound.

As noted above in Chapter 1, Newman's confidence in the *via media* was badly shaken when the bishops of the Church of England virtually repudiated his 'Catholic' interpretation of the Thirty-nine Articles. About the same time he began to doubt whether the Anglican communion could claim the mark of catholicity, which seemed to him to be better verified in the Church of Rome. The crucial question, then, was whether the Church of Rome, with its superior catholicity, could claim to possess the mark of apostolicity as well.

Convinced that the true Church must exist somewhere, Newman began to reconsider. Could not the teachings in the Council of Trent and the Creed of Pius IV be understood as authentic continuations of the process of dogmatization at work in the early councils? To test this hypothesis Newman engaged in the research and reflection that resulted in his *Essay on the Development of Christian Doctrine*.[53]

The *Essay* is not a brief for a kind of dogmatic Darwinism. From the very outset Newman opposes the 'transformist' view that Christianity is ever in flux and accommodates itself to the times.[54] For him it is axiomatic that the faith of the apostles must perdure. But in order to retain its vitality and ward off new errors, the living Church will sometimes have to articulate its faith in new ways.

Granted that development must occur, it must still be asked whether the new formulations are in accord with the ancient faith. To respond to this difficult question he proposed seven tests for authentic development:[55]

1. *Preservation of type.* Just as an adult keeps the same members and organs as the newborn child, so the Church and its teaching must always remain recognizably the same. If St. Athanasius or St.

Ambrose were to come suddenly to life, what communion would they take to be their own?[56]

2. *Continuity of principles.* In order to preserve its type, the Church must stand by its foundational principles. Newman lists nine such principles and then adds a tenth – the principle of development itself.[57] Among the nine are the principle of dogma, the sacramental principle, the priority of faith over reason, and the propriety of intellectual inquiry into the meaning of revelation. If any of these principles were abandoned, Christianity itself would be mutilated.

3. *Power of assimilation.* As a healthy organism builds itself up by ingesting food, so the Church takes in what is assimilable in the cultures it meets, and transforms what it appropriates. The Church and its faith have matured by interaction with the great civilizations of Greece and Rome.

4. *Logical sequence.* Certain truths, when believed and put into practice, are seen to imply other cognate truths. For example, the remission of sin in baptism calls for completion by a sacrament of forgiveness for post-baptismal sin. Newman's term 'logical sequence' is much broader in scope than formal inference of conclusions from premises, although Newman does not exclude deductive argument.

5. *Anticipation of its own future.* Some doctrines that did not receive formal recognition until relatively late were foreshadowed by the beliefs and practice of Christians of an earlier time; for example, the veneration of relics of the martyrs as a prelude to the invocation of saints.

6. *Conservative action on its past.* Does the new doctrine confirm or weaken adherence to the ancient faith? He contends, for example, that the doctrine of the Holy Trinity, rightly understood, does not undermine, but rather supports, the prior and more fundamental doctrine of monotheism.

7. *Chronic vigor.* A church that retains its youthful vigor in spite of its antiquity may be presumed to be authentic. Corruption by its very nature leads to stagnation and decay.

In proposing these seven tests Newman makes no claim that they cogently demonstrate the truth of Roman Catholicism. He restricts his attention to a specific point: did the modern developments in the Church of Rome violate the criteria? Could Newman overcome his own previous objections?

The book does not purport to be a complete examination of the history of dogma. Newman derives his tests from the patristic period, with which he was familiar. Pursuing his own reflections, he made no effort to survey other theories of development, such as those often attributed to Thomas Aquinas, Vasquez, Molina, Suarez, de Lugo, and Bañez, not to mention the more recent speculations of Johann Sebastian Drey and Johann Adam Möhler. Even without going into these matters, he wrote a very substantial treatise. As he did so, it became clear to him that, just as the developments of the first centuries were consonant with biblical revelation, so the more recent developments in Roman Catholicism, including those that he had attacked in his Anglo-Catholic phase, could be seen as authentic expressions of the Christian 'idea.' In the midst of the chapter on the seventh note, Newman abruptly ended his book. Having written enough to answer his own question, he made his profession of faith to Father Dominic Barberi.

Mariology

Newman's Mariology may be studied as an illustration of all the principles set forth in this chapter. His own teaching about Mary developed gradually from his early Anglican sermons, in which he shows a deep veneration toward her but refrains from clear dogmatic statements about her Immaculate Conception and her Assumption. In his *Essay on Development* he frequently uses the Church's teaching about Mary as an example to be tested by his seven criteria of authentic development. In his *Discourses to Mixed Congregations*, representing his early enthusiasm with Roman Catholic teaching, he devotes the two final chapters to Mary. And finally, in his *Letter to Pusey*, he responds in a firm but friendly manner to the objections of his former associate in the Oxford Movement.

Newman's Mariology is both scriptural and patristic. He does not argue from Scripture alone, but from Scripture read in the light of tradition. The early Fathers, beginning with Justin, depicted Mary as the 'Second Eve,' and this title becomes the fundamental principle of Newman's Mariology. Just as Eve was the 'mother of all the living' (Gen. 3:20), so Mary is the mother of all who live in the supernatural order of grace. Already in Genesis we have a prophetic assertion of the perpetual enmity between the seed of the women and the seed of the serpent (Gen. 3:15). Just as Eve was free from sin from the first moment of her personal existence, so Mary was, by a special privilege, exempted from the penalty of original sin, so that she could be a fitting temple for the incarnate Word of God. Eve, seduced by the words of the serpent, failed in faith and obedience. Mary believed the message of the angel and by her obedience brought about the redemption of the human race. Although Scripture maintains a reverent silence about Mary after the resurrection, the image of the mother, the child, and the serpent in the twelfth chapter of the Apocalypse of John affords a basis for the Christian doctrine that Mary has been taken up into heaven, where she intercedes with her Son for the Church militant, including Christians who neither know nor invoke her. In his *Discourses to Mixed Congregations* Newman defends the doctrine of the Assumption on the ground that Christ could not fittingly allow the flesh and blood from which his body were taken to molder in the grave.[58]

In the *Essay on Development* Mary appears principally in the discussion of two of the seven criteria – anticipation of the future (no. 5) and conservative action on the past (no. 6). In the Fathers, Newman concedes, we do not find a developed Marian doctrine, but Mary's virginity is extolled and imitated as a means of union with God; she is seen as actively involved in the process of redemption, and her medieval role as a patroness with clients is anticipated.[59]

In considering the sixth note Newman takes cognizance of the Protestant objection that the *cultus* of Mary draws the minds and hearts of Christians away from the more fundamental truth of their relationship to Christ. He replies that the contrary is true. The title *theotokos* (God-bearer) was bestowed on Mary

to protect the doctrine of the Incarnation and to preserve the faith of Catholics from a specious Humanitarianism. And if we take a survey at least of Europe, we shall find that it is not those religious communions which are characterized by devotion toward the Blessed Virgin that have ceased to adore her Eternal Son, but those very bodies ... which have renounced devotion to her. ... They who were accused of worshipping a creature in His stead, still worship Him; their accusers, who hoped to worship Him so purely, they, whenever obstacles to the development of their principles have been removed, have ceased to worship Him altogether.[60]

Newman's fullest discussion of the role of Mary appears in his *Letter to Pusey*. In the first half he restates, in a more systematic fashion, the main points of the *Essay on Development*. He emphasizes the Catholic doctrine that Mary is not a mere passive recipient of grace, but an active cooperator in the work of redemption. He points out that original sin is not in the Catholic view a positive stain but the absence of the gifts of grace. He insists that the Immaculate Conception is logically implied in the patristic view of Mary as the 'new Eve.' He argues that Christians who accept the invocation of saints, as Pusey does, should find no difficulty in turning to Mary, who already showed her intercessory role at Cana. In the second part of the book, Newman discusses the excesses and abuses that Pusey reprehends in Catholic practice. He admits that there are some excesses on the level of popular religion, but he does not find them in the official teaching and the publicly approved prayers of the Church. It is unnecessary, he says, to insist on minute accuracy in popular devotional writings.[61]

Interplay of history and dogma

Newman's views on Scripture, tradition, and dogma, worked out in substance before he became a Catholic, proved to be a blessing to the Church that he joined. Since the Council of Trent it had become rather common to view Scripture and tradition as two separate and parallel fonts. Newman saw the need to treat them as two facets of a single rule of faith. It was not as though some doctrines came from Scripture and others from tradition, but rather all doctrines have a foundation, more or less complete, in Scripture, but cannot be verified without the added insights offered by tradition.

In his writings on inspiration, Newman frankly faced up to the problem of historical and scientific inaccuracies in Scripture, and showed why these inaccuracies did not prevent Scripture from being an inspired guide, free from error in matters pertaining to salvation. He likewise came to terms with the troubled history of the canon in the early centuries.

With regard to tradition; Newman recognized the existence of traditions that might be laden with legendary features or marked by wishful thinking. But these traditions, which Newman called 'prophetical,' did not diminish the authority of the central Christian tradition, which he at one point called 'episcopal.' As he moved toward Catholicism, he saw that even the authoritative tradition was not static. Taking cognizance of dynamic developments, he anticipated the more flexible notion of tradition that was to prevail in the twentieth century.

Another major contribution was Newman's recognition that revelation was originally communicated as an encompassing 'idea' and only gradually, through reflection, came to be formulated in creedal and dogmatic propositions. While making due allowance for the historical situations that impelled the Church to formulate new dogmas, Newman gave no quarter to dogmatic relativism. He argued vigorously for the irreversibility of dogmas, not necessarily in their wording, but in their meaning. His balanced position represents a middle course between a fluid historicism and a rigid dogmatism.

Newman's *Essay on the Development of Christian Doctrine* is one of the most seminal works of nineteenth-century theology. A highly personal achievement, it bears the marks of having been written to solve the author's principal difficulty against accepting the Roman Catholic Church. The book should not be treated as though it aimed to present a finished theory. Newman, in fact, would have repudiated the notion that the development of doctrine could be reduced to a set of laws. He did think it possible, however, to propose some rules of thumb that could be applied by the discerning inquirer to distinguish between true developments and corruptions. This single work, far more than any other, established the idea of doctrinal development as a principle of Catholic theology. Although much has been written on the subject since Newman's time, it would be difficult to name any rival treatise that measures up to his in depth and thoroughness.

Notes

1   Newman, *The Arians of the Fourth Century* (London: Longmans, Green & Co., 1897), p. 79; hereafter abbreviated *Arians*.

2   Ibid., p. 80.

3   Newman, *Apologia pro Vita Sua* (London: Longmans, Green & Co., 1929), p. 1; hereafter abbreviated *Apol.*

4   Newman, *Certain Difficulties Felt by Anglicans in Catholic Teaching Considered*, 2 vols. (London: Longmans, Green & Co., 1908, 1910), vol. 2, p. 12, hereafter abbreviated *Diff.*; cf. Newman, *The Via Media of the Anglican Church* 2 vols. (London: Longmans, Green & Co., 1891), vol. 1, pp. 288–9, hereafter abbreviated *VM*.

5   *Arians*, p. 50; *VM*, vol. 1, p. 158.

6   *VM*, vol. 1, p. 132.

7   Ibid., p. 167.

8 *Arians*, pp. 50–51.

9 Newman, 'Holy Scripture in Its Relation to the Catholic Creed,' in his *Discussions and Arguments on Various Subjects* (London: Longmans, Green & Co., 1910), pp. 109–253, at pp. 110, 125; hereafter abbreviated *Disc*.

10 Newman, *An Essay on the Development of Christian Doctrine* (Notre Dame, IN.: University of Notre Dame Press, 1989), p. 59; hereafter abbreviated *Dev*.

11 *Arians*, p. 55

12 *VM*, vol. 1, p. 54.

13 'Quod ubique, quod semper, quod ab omnibus creditum est,' Vincent of Lerins, *Commonitorium*, p. 2.

14 *VM*, vol. 1, p. 55–6.

15 Ibid., pp. 249–50.

16 Ibid., p. 250.

17 This process of integration is explained in Günther Biemer, *Newman on Tradition* (New York: Herder & Herder, 1967), pp. 51–67.

18 *VM*, vol. 1, p. 291.

19 Ibid., p. 303.

20 'Inspiration in its Relation to Revelation,' in Newman, *On the Inspiration of Scripture*, ed. J. Derek Holmes and Robert Murray (Washington, DC: Corpus, 1967), pp. 101–28.

21 'Essay II;' ibid., pp. 145–6.

22 Holmes and Murray, 'Introduction,' ibid., p. 43.

23 On the exchange with Father Healy see 'Introduction,' ibid., pp. 37–47. Cf. the published version in Essay II, p. 153, with footnotes.

24 Such is the judgment of J. Seynaeve, 'Newman (Doctrine scripturaire du Cardinal),' *Dictionnaire de la Bible (Supplément)*, 6 (1960), cols. 427–74, at col. 445.

25 Vatican II, Dogmatic Constitution *Dei Verbum*, no. 11.

26 *Arians*, p. 56.

27 Ibid., p. 63.

28 *Arians*, pp. 404–5; cf. *Dev*., pp. 342–3.

29 *Arians*, p. 409.

30 Ibid., p. 410.

31 Newman, *Fifteen Sermons Preached before the University of Oxford 1826–43* (London: SPCK, 1970), p. 27; hereafter abbreviated *OUS*.

32 *Dev*., p. 36. As many scholars have noted, Newman is not perfectly consistent in his use of the term 'idea,' but in a given context it is possible to discern his general meaning. For discussion of the term see Nicholas Lash, *Newman on Development:*

The Search for an Explanation in History (Shepherdstown, W. Va.: Patmos, 1975), pp. 46–54, 168–9.

33   In the next few paragraphs I follow in substance what I have written in 'From Images to Truth: Newman on Revelation and Faith,' *Theological Studies* 51 (1990), pp. 252–67, at p. 254.

34   *OUS*, pp. 331–2.

35   Ibid., p. 322.

36   *Dev.*, p. 40.

37   Ibid., p. 357.

38   *Apol.*, p. 27.

39   Tract 73, 'On the Introduction of Rationalistic Principles into Revealed Religion,' *Essays Critical and Historical*, 2 vols. (London: Longmans, Green & Co., 1895), vol. 1, pp. 30–99, at p. 31.

40   *Arians*, p. 37.

41   Ibid., pp. 141–3.

42   Ibid., pp. 148–9.

43   *OUS*, pp. 312–51.

44   Ibid., p. 333.

45   Ibid., p. 332.

46   *Apol.*, p. 4–5.

47   Ibid., p. 48.

48   *Dev.*, p. 325.

49   Ibid., pp. 347–8.

50   Text in *Addresses to Cardinal Newman and His Replies*, ed. W. P. Neville (London: Longmans, Green & Co., 1905), pp. 61–70, at p. 64.

51   *Dev.*, pp. 357–8.

52   *Disc.*, pp. 128–9.

53   The *Essay on the Development of Christian Doctrine* exists in three editions, those of 1845, 1846, and 1878. The changes between the first two editions are minor. The third edition contains significant rearrangements of the material but, in Newman's own eyes, no substantial change in argument. Most of the verbal changes are, in the estimation of Owen Chadwick, 'tinkering' [*From Bossuet to Newman*, 2nd ed. (Cambridge: Cambridge University Press, 1987), p. 190]. This judgment is sustained by Charles F. Harrold in his article 'Newman's Revisions in the *Essay on the Development of Christian Doctrine*' in the edition that he introduced and edited (London: Longmans, Green & Co., 1949). For the sake of convenience, I shall consistently refer (as I have thus far) to the 1878 edition, reprinted by photostatic copy, Notre Dame, IN.: University of Notre Dame Press, 1989.

81

54   *Dev.*, pp. 10, 38.

55   Ibid., pp. 169–206. In the 1845 edition of the *Essay* Newman used the term 'tests' in his section headings, but in the 1878 edition he replaced it by 'notes.' In the text, however, he continued to speak of the 'notes' as 'tests.'

56   Ibid., pp. 97–8; cf. 321–2.

57   Ibid., pp. 325–6.

58   Newman, *Discourses to Mixed Congregations* (London: Longmans, Green & Co.,1893), p. 371.

59   *Dev.*, pp. 408–18.

60   Ibid, p. 426; cf. p. 202.

61   'A Letter Addressed to the Reverend E. B. Pusey on the Occasion of His *Eirenicon*,' in *Diff.*, vol. 2, pp. 1–170, at p. 101.

6

The Church as organ of revelation

Although Newman's greatest theological contributions were in the realms of theological epistemology and the development of Christian doctrine, he was also, to an eminent degree, a theologian of the Church. From the time that he began to preach and write in the field of theology, he never had any doubt that revealed truth and grace were transmitted in and through the Church. His only question was where the true Church was to be found.

The Church: visible, apostolic, catholic

For Newman's basic idea of the Church one can scarcely do better than consult his *Parochial and Plain Sermons* and his *Sermons Bearing on Subjects of the Day*, written during his years at Oxford. A recurrent theme in these sermons is the nature of the Church as both visible and invisible. 'The word Church,' he writes, 'applied to the body of Christians in this world, means but one thing in Scripture, a visible body invested with invisible privileges. Scripture does not speak of two bodies, one visible, the other invisible, each with its own complement of members. But this is the common notion at present; and it is an erroneous, and (I will add) a dangerous notion.'[1]

In its visible aspect, says Newman, the Church is identical with the Kingdom proclaimed and established in history by Jesus Christ. Unlike the majority of theologians today, Newman does not distinguish between the Church and the Kingdom of God. 'If we will be scriptural in our view of the Church,' writes Newman, 'we must consider that it is a kingdom, that its officers have great powers and high gifts, that they are charged with the custody of Divine Truth, that they are all united together, and that the nations are subject to them.'[2] Apostolic in its beginnings, it remains so today. 'Much and rightly as we reverence old lineage, noble birth, and illustrious ancestry, yet the royal dynasty of the Apostles is far older than all the kingly families which are now on the earth. Every Bishop of the Church whom we behold is a lineal descendant of St. Peter and St. Paul after the order of a spiritual birth.'[3] Throughout the remainder of his life Newman continued to hold that the true Church must be governed by bishops in the apostolic succession and must preserve the apostolic faith undefiled. But, as we shall see, he came to believe that the Church of England had not preserved this apostolic succession in ministry and doctrine.

The Church as a visible society might be called not only a kingdom but also an empire, because it knows no boundaries. 'The great object of Christ's coming was to subdue the world, to claim it as His own, to assert His rights over it as its Master, to destroy the usurped dominion of the enemy.'[4] Although the sins of the members have to some degree thwarted Christ's design that all the nations of the earth should be subject to his gentle rule, the Church in fact exercises a spiritual sovereignty that in extent and duration exceeds any of the world's empires, past and present, including that of Rome.[5] For Newman the Church, like the British Empire, includes many states; it exercises dominion not only over its immediate subjects but over the rulers of other kingdoms; it is engaged in perpetual warfare against its enemies; seeking to conquer them, it sometimes advances and at other times retreats.[6]

The Church, of course, differs radically from every earthly kingdom.

Earthly kingdoms are founded, not in justice, but in injustice. They are created by the sword, by robbery, cruelty, perjury, craft, and fraud. There never was a kingdom, except Christ's, which was not conceived and born, nurtured and educated, in sin. ... But ... the life of the Church lies, not in inflicting evil, but in receiving it; not in doing, but in suffering; in all those things which the world despises, as being fitter in themselves to pull down an empire than to build it up; in patience, in simplicity, in innocence, in concession, in passiveness, in resignation.[7]

Through gentleness and charity, the Church has attained the universality, or catholicity, to which all earthly empires have aspired in vain.[8]

Visible in its government and sacraments, the Church is invisible by reason of her vital principle and the vast majority of her members, who no longer belong to our company here on earth.[9] The visible body is the part that can be seen and pointed out: a type or sign of the interior kingdom that will endure forever. The visible is continually dying, but the invisible body keeps increasing.[10] The sacraments and ministries of the Church are means of entry and growth; they are steps, as it were, leading to Christ's throne.[11] In this visible Church, which has the successors of the apostles as its rulers and all professing Christian people as its members, the Church invisible is gradually molded and matured.[12]

In an almost Platonic fashion, Newman can assert: 'This *invisible* body is the *true* Church, because it changes not, even though it keeps increasing.'[13] The invisible dimension of the Church is for him closely connected with its catholicity. Properly speaking, he says, the Church is not here on earth, except insofar as the dead may be said to be present here among us, or as heaven is. The new Jerusalem dwells in the visible churches of every land, fully and entirely, as the human soul is present in every part of the body.[14] In the Church the unseen world of grace and glory encroaches upon this world. The visible manifestations of the Church are totally dependent upon the invisible.[15] The visible temple is but the occasional and partial manifestation of the unseen: 'A Temple with God for its Light, and Christ for the High Priest, with wings of Angels for its arches, with Saints and Teachers for its pillars, and with worshippers for its pavement.'[16]

From the nature of the Church, her purpose may easily be deduced. Although the Church has raised the tone of morals and benefited human society in countless ways, her true purpose is to deliver her members out of this present evil world and raise them beyond the capacities of their own nature. In a sermon with the title 'The Visible Church for the Sake of the Elect' Newman insists that the aim of all Paul's labors and sufferings was not that he might civilize the world or cultivate human abilities but that he might bring souls to glory.[17] The real object of the gospel is to produce saints, few though they may be, rather than to be useful for any worldly purpose.[18]

The Church: holy and one

The Church is holy with a holiness that she cannot lose. Newman takes quite literally the statements of Holy Scripture that the Church was from her beginnings and remains today 'the pillar and the ground of the Truth, the Mother of us all, the House of God, the dwelling-place of the Holy Ghost, the Spouse of Christ, a glorious Church without spot or wrinkle or any such thing.'[19] In spite of the sins of many of her members, she remains 'all glorious within, in that inward shrine, made up of faithful hearts, and inhabited by the Spirit of grace.'[20]

Newman is aware of the objection that the visible Church cannot be the true Church because it contains sinners. Rather than saying, as the objectors do, that bad men cannot be members of the true Church, he prefers to say: 'Bad men cannot be true members of the Church.'[21] They are like dead branches on a living tree. Because they are spiritually dead, it does not follow that the Church of which they are members is also dead.[22] Individuals may forfeit the privileges of membership, but the beloved Spouse of Christ retains the spiritual gifts that were conferred upon her.[23]

When discussing the marks by which the true Church is to be recognized, Newman in these sermons and elsewhere relies more on catholicity, apostolicity, and unity than on holiness. The Church does of course foster holiness in her members, but the saintly life tends to be unostentatious, while evil 'flaunts itself and is loud.'[24]

Thus far we have dealt tangentially, as Newman himself does in these sermons, with the Church as holy, catholic, and apostolic. It remains for us to discuss its unity. Newman is clear throughout the *Parochial and Plain Sermons* in holding that the types and prophecies in the Old Testament refer to a single elect people, which is the Church by another name. Ezekiel predicts that God will set up one Shepherd to feed his flock.[25] In the Song of Solomon the Bridegroom declares: 'My undefiled is but one; she is the only one of her mother, she is the elect of her that bare her.'[26] The Angel Gabriel announces that the King to be born of Mary is destined to reign over the house of Jacob forever.[27]

In a sermon on 'The Unity of the Church'[28] Newman cites a multiplicity of texts from Paul and John to the effect that the Church is and must be one. It is one body, one flock, one mystical Temple. By baptism we are all brought into the one body, which is governed by the successors of the apostles. No one can enter into the sacramental ministry without being ordained by members of this apostolic body. It follows, therefore, that Christians ought to live together in a single visible society here on earth, 'not as a confused unconnected multitude, but united and organized one with another, by an established order, so as evidently to appear and to act as one.'[29] Beyond these rather general statements, Newman does not in these sermons inquire into the kind and degree of unity that could be found in the Church of his day.

In his 1837 work, *The Prophetical Office of the Church*, Newman probes further into the question of unity. After acknowledging that there is lamentable doctrinal confusion in the English church, he replies that the Roman church during the Middle Ages was in great spiritual confusion, amounting at times to schism among parties supporting rival claimants to the See of Rome. Thus the Roman communion itself is not exempt from the troubles that always afflict the Church of Christ.[30]

Soon after he became a Catholic, Newman replied to his own previous objections in *Certain Difficulties Felt by Anglicans in Catholic Teaching*. He pointed out that schismatic movements within the Catholic fold died out quickly, so that unity of doctrine was soon restored. The national church of England, by contrast, 'is no guide into the truth, because no one knows what it holds, and what it commands: one party says this, and a second party says that, and a third party says neither this nor that.'[31] Newman eventually concluded, therefore, that the mark of unity tells strongly in favor of the Roman communion. In a private letter of 1852 he asserted that the Branch Theory was absurd, because bodies that had broken off communion with one another could not constitute a single Church. 'If the Church be a kingdom, a body politic, visibly, it is impossible that both the Roman and the Anglican communion can be that one body politic because they are two distinct bodies.'[32] At least one of them must be in schism.

The prophetical office

Returning to Newman's pre-Catholic period, we may now consider more fully his *Lectures on the Prophetical Office*, his most thematic treatment of the Church. In his Introduction he notes that most Englishmen profess no clear doctrine of the Church. Considering comfort in religion to lie in all questions being open, they make no effort to determine the meaning of the article in the Creed professing faith in one, holy, catholic, and apostolic Church.[33] So far have Protestants neglected the meaning of the term that to speak of the Church at all is thought to savor of Rome.[34] Non-Roman Christians who write on the Church, therefore, are obliged to explain why they are not Romanists and how they differ from Rome. Newman's *Lectures*, therefore, will inevitably seem to be directed against Rome, but their main object is not controversy but edification. If the Roman view of the Church is not true, members of the English Church are obliged in very shame to state what they themselves hold.[35]

As the title indicates, the *Lectures on the Prophetical Office* deal only with one aspect of the Church. By the 'prophetical office' Newman means the teaching function of the Church, its capacity and obligation to transmit the apostolic faith to all generations. In great part the book goes over much of the same ground we have covered in the discussion of Scripture, tradition, and doctrine in Chapter 5. Writing here from an Anglican perspective, Newman is seeking to find a *via media* between what he regards as Protestant and Roman deviations.

As we have seen in our discussion of tradition, Newman distinguishes between the apostolic and the prophetic. 'Apostles,' he says, 'rule and preach; Prophets expound.'[36] In the *Prophetical Office* he actually deals more with the apostolic or episcopal office than with the prophetic in this narrower sense. He considers the prophetic tradition to be binding only to the extent that it agrees with, and interprets, the apostolic.

The Protestant position, as Newman portrays it, accepts Scripture alone as the norm. He has no difficulty in showing that if you put the Bible into the hands of theologically uneducated persons, you can hardly expect them to come up with an orthodox version of the faith. All the major heresies have had plausible biblical grounds. Since the Bible was never intended to serve as an adequate source of doctrine, it must be read in the light of tradition. The Bible itself affords ample testimony that the Church is the 'pillar and the ground of the truth' (1 Tim. 3:15) and that the apostles and their successors are the authorized teachers of revealed doctrine.

Against Protestantism, therefore, and in agreement with Rome, Newman in these lectures maintains that the Church has an authoritative teaching office, exercised by the bishops as successors of the apostles. Following the norm of St. Vincent of Lerins, he holds that all are bound to believe everything that the bishops teach constantly and unanimously as the Catholic faith. Among the articles of belief Newman gives pride of place to those listed in the creeds of the early Church, including the Athanasian Creed.

In the *Prophetical Office*, however, Newman takes pains to differentiate his position from that of the Roman Church. Rome, he believes, goes astray by exalting the teaching authority of the pope to the point where it trumps all other sources of doctrine. The Fathers, for Roman theologians, have authority only to the extent that they agree with what the modern popes teach. The Roman Church therefore violates the rule of catholicity by canonizing the particular tenets of one part of the Church and demanding that her members submit abjectly to the pope as an infallible teacher.

Newman in these pages makes a distinction between infallibility and indefectibility. By infallibility he seems to mean a guarantee of truth attaching to the pronouncements of a particular office: they are deemed to be true just because they issue from that office with the required authentication. Newman finds no adequate evidence that Christ has equipped the Church with this prerogative. But he contends that the Church, without claiming infallibility, can expect the confidence and obedience of her members.[37] The Church is indefectible because she will always teach the essentials of the faith, as she has done in the past. She has the supernatural gifts needed to transmit the apostolic faith and to condemn errors opposed to it. The promise that the Church will always remain the pillar and ground of truth, and that the gates of hell will never prevail against her, is satisfied by the consensus that continues to exist on fundamental doctrines in all branches of the Catholic Church. Newman considers it evident that the Church of England is part of the Church Catholic.

The essentials of the faith, Newman believes, were set forth by the creeds of the early Church (including the *Quicumque* attributed to Athanasius) and by the dogmas of the early Councils, enacted before the division between Greeks and Latins. He attaches no great importance to setting some date beyond which councils would no longer be binding. His criterion is rather whether the council expresses the faith held by all Catholic Christians. Everything that Anglican Catholics teach as belonging to the apostolic deposit of faith is accepted by Roman Catholics as well.

Newman concedes that something has been lost by the divisions of Christians against one another. If the Church had remained united it might indeed be infallible, but in her divided state she does not enjoy her privileges in the fullest sense.[38] Like God's promises to Israel, his promises to the Church remain to some degree conditional on human cooperation. In spite of human infidelity, however, God will not allow the fundamental truth of the gospel to perish.

Newman does not accuse the papacy of officially teaching error but only of going beyond what is of faith by canonizing theological opinions about matters such as transubstantiation, the intercession of saints, the privileges of Mary, purgatory, indulgences, and the universal jurisdiction of the pope. These doctrines, he believes, are poorly grounded in Scripture and apostolic tradition, and for that reason ought not to be exalted into articles of faith. He regards the decrees of Trent and the Creed of Pius IV as over-restrictive.

The Roman error, at root, is a sense of compulsion to present a complete system of doctrine as the object of faith. The assent of faith, for Roman Catholics, seems to be directed to an organized body of knowledge, with all its components clearly spelled out. Envisaged in this way, Christianity loses its mysterious character. When faith is depicted as an obligatory submission to a system of doctrine, the personal relationship to the divine Author of faith is obscured, and holiness is deprived of its native freshness and vigor.[39]

Such, then, are some of the doctrinal objections that Newman the Anglo-Catholic raises against the Roman Church. In later works he will respond to these objections, especially by making the case for infallibility in three major works: the *Essay on Development*, the *Apologia*, and the *Letter to the Duke of Norfolk*.

The *Essay on Development*

In the *Essay on Development* Newman has a powerful section on the 'antecedent probability' of infallibility. Revelation itself, he argues, comes to us with a profession of infallibility. If God speaks, his word cannot be false. The common sense of mankind 'feels that the very idea of revelation implies a present informant and guide, and that an infallible one.'[40] The revelation could not long survive in its purity and fullness without an authority that was protected against error. Protestants tend to regard the Bible as such an infallible authority, but Newman has shown that the inspired Scriptures were not intended and are not suited to fulfill that purpose by themselves alone. Thus we are left with the question of Peter in the Gospel: 'Lord, to whom shall we go?' (Jn 6:68). Scripture, as we have seen, refers to the Church as 'the pillar and ground of the truth' and promises that the Spirit will be with her to the end of time (cf. Is. 59:21). Everything therefore conspires to persuade us that Christ will supply an organ of truth, to whose judgment we may securely submit. 'If Christianity is both social and dogmatic, and intended for all ages, it must humanly speaking have an infallible expounder.'[41]

Believing as he does in the development of doctrine, Newman applies the principle of development to the papal office itself. A good foundation, he notes, is provided by the New Testament, especially in the Petrine texts of Matthew 16:18, Luke 22:32, and John 21:15–17. But the Fathers of the first two centuries, he concedes, are relatively silent on the subject. In the third century, however, Cyprian and Firmilian attest the idea that the primacy lives on in the pope as Peter's successor. In the fourth century Julius, Athanasius, Damasus, Jerome, Siricius, and Optatus increasingly emphasize the prerogatives of the papacy, preparing the way for the fuller doctrine set forth in the fifth century by Innocent, Augustine, Celestine, Prosper, Leo, and Peter Chrysologus. The development in teaching about the papacy, Newman finds, conforms to the criteria of the *Essay* for discerning authentic developments.

In light of this finding, Newman revisits some of the difficulties raised in *The Prophetical Office*. The Anglican position, he finds, is inconsistent. If one insists on explicit early testimonies, one ought not to credit the doctrines of original sin and the Real Presence in the Eucharist, which Anglicans nevertheless hold. But if one affirms these teachings one should, on similar grounds, accept the primacy of the pope in teaching and governing the universal Church. Indeed, the doctrine of the Trinity itself is poorly attested by the Ante-Nicene Fathers, many of whom are Arian or Semi-Arian in their language about the Son, while they give little attention to the divinity of the Holy Spirit.[42]

Particularly impressive is Newman's account of the role of Leo I in connection with the Council of Chalcedon. He describes the mighty force of the Eutychian heresy, which nearly prevailed as dogma in a moderate Monophysite form. 'If the East could determine a matter of faith independently of the West, certainly the Monophysite heresy was established as Apostolic truth in all its provinces from Macedonia to Egypt.'[43] But Pope Leo, with the support of the Emperor Marcian and several distinguished theologians such as Chrysologus and Theodoret, turned the tide. The situation of the Church in Newman's day was similar to that in the fifth century. 'Heresies are rife and bishops negligent within its own pale ... there is but one Voice for whose decision the peoples wait with trust, one Name and one See to which they look with hope, and that name Peter, and that see Rome.'[44]

The *Essay* does not purport to be a full answer to all the objections raised in the *Prophetical Office*, but it does at various points touch on issues such as Purgatory, indulgences, devotion to Mary, and the intercession of saints. On all these points Newman finds the current teaching of the Church to be a reasonable and logical development of other well-established doctrines.

The *Apologia*

Twenty years later, in his *Apologia*, Newman returned to the theme of infallibility. His treatment here is brief but rhetorically powerful. The Bible as a book, he says, 'cannot make a stand against the wild living intellect of man.'[45] Hence it is by no means improbable that if God wants to keep his revelation alive in spite of the energy of human skepticism, he might introduce a power invested with the prerogative of infallibility.[46] The Church's infallibility, Newman points out, is restricted within certain bounds. 'The great truths of the moral law, of natural religion, and of Apostolic faith, are both its boundary and its foundation.'[47] In the first edition Newman then added the following sentence, deleted from subsequent editions: 'Thus, in illustration, [infallibility] does not extend to statements, however sound and evident, which are mere logical conclusions from the Articles of the Apostolic *Depositum*; again, it can pronounce nothing about the persons of heretics, whose works fall within its legitimate province.' In a letter of 1868 to Father John Stanislas Flanagan, Newman explains that this sentence, reflecting the opinion of Philipp Neri Chrismann, seemed to take a position on a disputed question that Newman preferred to leave open.[48]

In a later letter to Flanagan, Newman affirmed as his personal opinion that logical deductions from the deposit of faith could be made portions of the Church's dogma, but he did not propose this view as a matter of faith.[49] In his diaries and private correspondence he frequently raised the question whether dogmatic facts, such as the heretical character of Jansen's work, or the fact that a given pope or council was legitimate, could be matters of faith. He leaned toward the view that infallibility extended 'indirectly' to matters such as these, insofar as they served to give concrete form to the truth of revelation.[50] He was unwilling to say that such truths were to be believed on a motive of 'ecclesiastical faith,' a term that seemed to him to imply that the Church could exact faith in her own word. For matters indirectly pertaining to the revealed deposit he preferred to speak of acquiescence through a reverence stemming from faith (*pietas fidei*).[51]

In the *Apologia* Newman disclaims any intent to determine

anything about the essential seat of infallibility 'because that is a question doctrinal, not historical and practical.'[52] But several pages later he mentions that the case of the Immaculate Conception, defined by the Pope in 1854 on his own authority, is exceptional because 'It is to the Pope in Ecumenical Council that we look, as the normal seat of infallibility.'[53] When Pius IX announced his intention of calling an ecumenical council, Newman expected that the Council would be asked to ratify the definition of 1854.

When Vatican I directed its attention to the theme of papal infallibility, Newman was somewhat alarmed. He hoped that the question whether the pope was infallible in acting alone, rather than in council or with the consent of the universal Church, would be left open to theological debate. He feared that a definition of papal infallibility, promulgated without the desirable restrictions, would alienate many Catholics and needlessly deepen the gulf between Catholics and other Christians. In a letter to his own bishop, William Ullathorne of Birmingham, of January 28, 1870 he gave vivid expression to his fears.

> What have we done to be treated, as the faithful never were treated before? When has definition of doctrine de fide been a luxury of devotion, and not a stern painful necessity? Why should an aggressive insolent faction be allowed to 'make the heart of the just to mourn, whom the Lord hath not made sorrowful?' Why can't we be let alone, when we have pursued peace, and thought no evil? I assure you, my dear Lord, some of the truest minds are driven one way and another, and do not know where to rest their feet; one day determining to give up all theology as a bad job, and recklessly to believe henceforth all the worst which a book like Janus[54] says; others doubting about the capacity possessed by Bishops, drawn from all corners of the earth, to judge what is fitting for European society, and then again angry with the Holy See for listening to the flattery of a clique of Jesuits, Redemptorists, and converts.[55]

When Newman actually saw the text of the definition in July, his anxiety was somewhat quieted. He was pleased with its moderation and felt personally able to accept it. But he still believed that there were reasons why a Catholic might suspend judgment on the validity of the definition. In particular, he noted that while the Constitution was approved by 533 votes in favor and only two opposed, more than eighty departed from Rome before the final vote, thereby signifying their opposition.[56] A mere majority of the Council, he believed, rather than a moral unanimity, could not enact dogmatic decrees. If the opposition had continued and solidified, Newman might well have doubted the validity of the definition. But the opposition quickly melted away. The opposing bishops submitted, and the vast majority of the faithful likewise accepted the definition. The conciliar decrees were thus ratified by their reception. Although some few joined with Professor Ignaz von Döllinger in a protest movement, which eventually led to the formation of the 'Old Catholic' church, their dissenting stance could only be defended by a denial of the principle of development or by an extreme interpretation of the Vatican text that Newman found untenable.[57] The follow-up of Vatican I thus confirmed Newman in his opinion that the adequate subject of infallibility was the Church as a whole – the united episcopate under the pope, together with the theologians and the faithful as a body.

The *Letter to the Duke of Norfolk*

For several years Newman made no public statement about the dogmatic definitions of the First Vatican Council. He was moved to break his official silence when the liberal former Prime Minister, William E. Gladstone, wrote an *Expostulation* against the Vatican Decrees, interpreting them, in the context of Pius IX's *Syllabus of Errors*, as a ploy to regain temporal power. Urged on by several friends, Newman undertook a reply.

Although ostensibly writing against Gladstone, Newman was using him as an occasion to promote his own moderate interpretation of the Council against intransigent Ultramontanes such as William George Ward. In his *Letter to the Duke of Norfolk* he followed essentially the same line as the German Bishop Joseph Fessler, whose *True and False Infallibility* had just been translated into English by Newman's fellow-Oratorian, Ambrose St. John. Fessler, who enjoyed great prestige as the Secretary General of the Council, exemplified what Newman called a 'wise and gentle minimism.'[58]

Before expounding the conciliar text itself, Newman in his *Letter* took up a number of historical questions raised by his adversary. Gladstone's charge that the Church of Rome was repudiating ancient history affords Newman with an occasion to depict the papacy as the legitimate heir of the 'ecumenical hierarchy' of the fourth century. He then points out that the spiritual allegiance of

Catholics to the pope does not undermine their loyalty to the Civil Power. In a brilliant chapter on conscience he shows that Gladstone is unwarranted in holding that the Catholic's allegiance to the pope overrides the believer's personal responsibility. And then, as the immediate background for Vatican I, he devotes two scintillating chapters to the Encyclical *Quanta cura* and the *Syllabus of Errors* appended to it – the latter being a compilation of earlier papal teachings assembled by an anonymous author. While defending the propositions in the *Syllabus* taken in the context of the Pope's writings from which they were culled, Newman makes it clear that he despised the recklessness of the 'circles of light-minded men in his city who were laying bets with each other whether the Syllabus would 'make a row in Europe' or not.'[59] It was irresponsible, he felt, to kindle the flame that he and others were now being asked to put out. Thus his defense of the *Syllabus* is in part a criticism of it.

The book concludes with two chapters on Vatican I and its Decrees. In opposition to Gladstone, Newman contends that the Council taught only a very moderate doctrine of infallibility, limiting it to statements of faith and morals that the pope issued from the chair of Peter (*ex cathedra Petri*) with the intention of binding every member of the Church to accept his judgment with a definitive assent. While Newman was able to accept the dogma as a close reading of the text requires, he considered that the definition presented only one aspect of infallibility. The role of the pope still needed to be seen in relation to other elements in the Church. In his letters Newman consoled his friends by pointing out that doctrine normally develops by a dialectical process, involving an alternation between different facets. Just as the Christology of Ephesus was to be cured of its one-sidedness by the teaching of Chalcedon, so too, Newman predicted, it would fall to the lot of a future council to 'trim the boat' offsetting the imbalances of the late Vatican Council.[60] Many commentators consider that Vatican II fulfilled this prophecy of Newman.

Constancy and variation

Throughout all the variations we have seen in this chapter, Newman's thought remained constant on certain points. The organic and sacramental ecclesiology set forth in his Anglican sermons remained with him throughout his career. He never wavered in his conviction that the Church of Christ is a visible society, one, holy, catholic, and apostolic. From his boyhood, he firmly maintained that the revelation of Christ contained determinate truths to be proclaimed by the Church throughout all ages. While writing his treatise on the *Development of Doctrine* he became convinced that the 'additions' to the ancient faith in modern Roman Catholicism were legitimate developments, not corruptions or accretions. From then on he became one of the chief defenders of infallibility, though, as we have seen, he was slow to make up his mind about the seat and the scope of infallibility in the Church.

Newman's personal correspondence during and immediately after the First Vatican Council gives a fascinating disclosure of the mind of the theologian at work. He is manifestly torn because he considers it pastorally unwise to proclaim the infallibility of the pope speaking outside of a general council. But he personally believes the doctrine and eventually reconciles himself to the proclamation. Because he was so sensitive to the difficulties, his defense of the dogma had special credibility. His final position on the seat and scope of infallibility stands up well under examination more than a century later. Vatican II was to complete the work of Vatican I by stating more explicitly that the pope has no other infallibility than that which was given to the universal Church and is expressed by the consensus of the bishops.

Notes

1   Newman, *Parochial and Plain Sermons*, one-volume edition (San Francisco: Ignatius, 1987) 3:16, p. 617; hereafter abbreviated *PPS*.

2   Newman, *Sermons Bearing on Subjects of the Day* (London: Longmans, Green & Co., 1891), p. 227. This work, a reprint of the first edition of 1843, hereafter abbreviated *SSD*.

3   *PPS*, 3:17, p. 633.

4   *PPS*, 6:20, p. 1352.

5   *PPS*, 2:21, pp. 380, 383, 385.

6   *SSD*, p. 234.

7   *SSD*, p. 243.

8   *SSD*, p. 248.

9   *PPS*, 4:11, p. 834.

10 Ibid., p. 835.

11 Ibid., p. 836.

12   *PPS*, 3:17, pp. 629–30.

13   *PPS*, 4:11, p. 835.

14   Ibid.

15   Ibid., p. 837.

16   *PPS*, 6:20, p. 1350.

17   *PPS*, 4:10, pp. 820–1.

18   Ibid., p. 825–6.

19   *PPS*, 3:16, p. 624.

20   *PPS*, 2:8, pp. 284–5.

21   *PPS*, 3:16, p. 621.

22   Ibid., p. 622.

23   Ibid., p. 621.

24   JHN to John Rickards Mozley, 19 April 1874, *The Letters and Diaries of John Henry Newman* (London: Nelson, 1961–72, and Oxford: Clarendon, 1977–), 27:55, hereafter abbreviated *LD*. See Edward Jeremy Miller, *John Henry Newman on the Idea of the Church* (Shepherdstown, W. Va.: Patmos, 1987), pp. 50–1.

25   *PPS*, 2:8, p. 282 quoting Ezek. 34:23.

26   Ibid., p. 284, quoting Song of Songs 6:9; cf. 4:7.

27   Ibid., p. 282, quoting Lk. 1:32–3, 35.

28   *PPS*, 7:17, pp. 1538–45.

29   Ibid., p. 1540.

30   Newman, 'On the Fortunes of the Church,' *Lectures on the Prophetical Office of the Church Viewed Relatively to Romanism and Popular Protestantism*, Lecture XIV, pp. 331–55. I quote from the third edition, which Newman republished as volume 1 of *The Via Media of the Anglican Church* (London: Longmans, Green & Co., 1877), as reprinted in 1891.

31   Newman, *Certain Difficulties Felt by Anglicans in Catholic Teaching Considered*, 2 vols. (London: Longmans, Green & Co., 1908, 1910), vol. 1, p. 310, hereafter abbreviated *Diff.*

32   JHN to Lord Charles Thynne, 3 February 1852, *LD*, vol. 15, p. 27.

33   *Diff.*, vol. 1, pp. 3–4.

34   Ibid., p. 5.

35   Ibid., pp. 6–7.

36   *VM*, vol. 1, p. 250.

37   Ibid., p. 143.

38   Ibid., pp. 201–2.

39   Ibid., pp. 83–105.

40   Newman, *An Essay on the Development of Christian Doctrine* (Notre Dame, IN.: University of Notre Dame, 1989), p. 87.

41   Ibid., p. 90.

42   Ibid., pp. 14–18.

43   Ibid., p. 306.

44   Ibid., p. 322.

45   Newman, *Apologia pro Vita Sua* (London: Longmans, Green & Co., 1929), p. 245; hereafter abbreviated *Apol.*

46   Ibid.

47   Ibid., p. 253.

48   See *The Theological Papers of John Henry Newman on Biblical Inspiration and on Infallibility*, ed. J. Derek Holmes (Oxford: Clarendon, 1979), p. 113. I shall reproduce in this chapter some materials from Avery Dulles, 'Newman on Infallibility,' *Theological Studies* 51 (1990), pp. 434–49, at p. 446.

49   *Theological Papers on Biblical Inspiration and on Infallibility*, pp. 154–5.

50   Ibid., pp. 119, 141.

51   Ibid., pp. 146, 155.

52   *Apol.*, p. 249.

53   Ibid., p. 256.

54   Janus was one of the pseudonyms under which the German historian Ignaz von Döllinger wrote against the proceedings of the First Vatican Council. Some of the Janus letters were published in English in 1869 under the title *The Pope and the Council.*

55   *LD* vol. 25, pp. 18–19. For the larger context see John R. Page, *What Will Dr. Newman Do? John Henry Newman and Papal Infallibility 1865–1875* (Collegeville, MN: Liturgical Press, 1994), pp. 84–6.

56   Accounts vary on the number of minority bishops who left Rome before the final vote. John T. Ford gives the figure 'some sixty' in his article on Vatican Council I in *The New Dictionary of Theology* (Wilmington, Del.: Michael Glazier, 1987), pp. 1069–72 at p. 1072.

57   JHN to Alfred Plummer, 12 March and 3 April 1871; *LD*, vol. 25, pp. 301–2, 308–10.

58   Newman, 'Letter to the Duke of Norfolk,' in *Diff.*, vol. 2, pp. 171–378, at p. 339.

59   Ibid., pp. 297–8.

60   Ibid., pp. 306–7; cf. JHN to Alfred Plummer 3 April 1871, *LD*, vol. 25, pp. 308–10.

7

The roles of theologians and the laity

In the preceding chapter we have surveyed Newman's views on the role of popes and bishops in preserving, interpreting, and developing the apostolic deposit of faith. The hierarchical magisterium, for him, was an essential factor in the transmission of faith, but it never operated alone. The Church included theologians and lay persons, who likewise had active roles to play.

Theology vis-à-vis the magisterium

In seeking to grasp the proper relationships between the hierarchical magisterium, the theologians, and the lay faithful, Newman found himself faced with the question of authority and private judgment, which seriously concerned him both in his Anglican years and later as a Catholic. He solved the question for himself by applying the kind of dialectic he had previously worked out for the problem of faith and reason in the *Oxford University Sermons*.

In the *Prophetical Office* Newman seeks to find an Anglican *via media* between two extremes. Protestants, he alleges, consider that every individual has the right of deciding from Scripture what is Gospel truth, whereas Roman Catholics, on the contrary, hold that 'there is no subject in religious faith and conduct on which the Church may not pronounce a decision, such as to supersede the private judgment, and compel the assent, of every one of her members.'[1] Newman carves out an intermediate position by distinguishing between fundamental and secondary truths. The constitutive tradition, taught by bishops, is not subject to discussion, but the prophetical tradition, which is primarily interpretative, does not have the same binding force except where it coincides with the episcopal tradition.[2] In the category of necessary and fundamental doctrines resting on apostolic testimony Newman placed the Trinity, the Incarnation, the Atonement, original sin, the necessity of regeneration, the supernatural grace of the sacraments, the apostolic succession, the obligation of faith and obedience, and the eternity of future punishment.[3] Secondary doctrines, those that are not a part of this unchanging apostolic tradition and have no necessary bearing on salvation, could be believed or not according to the private judgment of the individual believer.[4]

During his last years as an Anglican Newman abandoned the distinction between fundamental and secondary doctrines. He began to see that the apostolic tradition is not a static thing, but that it develops under the aegis of the Church, which can authoritatively declare newly found implications of that tradition. Although believers are not free to repudiate the magisterium, private judgment is operative in their assessment of the credibility, meaning, and force of ecclesiastical pronouncements.

In his *Essay on the Development of Christian Doctrine* Newman discusses the interplay of dogma, faith, and theology. Dogma presents the revealed truth in language that is definitive and binding on the faithful; faith is the absolute acceptance of the divine word as it comes to us through the Church; theology conducts an intellectual inquiry into the dogmatic heritage and builds up a science of religion.[5] While commending docile submission to the word of God, Newman cautions that beliefs are not to be thoughtlessly professed with the tongue but intelligently held.[6] Intellectual honesty may require that a person take time before saying Yes even to the most solemn proclamation. The life of the *schola*, for Newman, consists in loving inquisitiveness about the grounds for, and the meaning and implications of, revealed truth. From the beginnings of Christianity, he says, reason has ever been awake in the Church. It rose to great heights in the golden age of the patristic theology and in the universities of medieval Europe.[7]

In his Catholic career Newman continued to ponder the dialectical interplay between ecclesiastical authority and private judgment. In his *Apologia* he raises against himself the objection that the infallibility of the magisterium brings order into reason only by destroying it.[8] But such, he says, is far from being the case.

> Every exercise of Infallibility is brought out into act by an intense and varied operation of the Reason, both as its ally and as its opponent, and provokes again, when it has done its work, a re-action of Reason against it; and, as in the civil polity the State exists and endures by means of the rivalry and collision, the encroachments and defeats of its constituent parts, so in like manner Catholic Christendom is no simple exhibition of religious absolutism, but presents a continuous picture of Authority and Private Judgment alternately advancing and retreating as the ebb and flow of the tide.[9]

The whole history of theology, according to Newman, refutes the supposition that infallibility places individual Catholics before the alternatives of slavish superstition and secret rebellion of heart.[10] It is individuals, not the Holy See, who have normally taken the initiative in theological inquiry. Only two of the popes (Leo and Gregory) have been doctors of the Church. Often enough councils have been guided by the genius of individuals, such as the deacon Athanasius at Nicaea, the Benedictine archbishop Anselm at Bari, and the Jesuit Alfonso Salmeron at Trent, all of whom prevailed by the force of their arguments rather than by the authority of office.[11]

Although we think of the Middle Ages as theocratic, it was a time when the intellect of the educated class was singularly restless. Individual theologians felt the freedom to propose their opinions for discussion, trusting in the processes of debate. Ideas were tested in the schools for generations before they were adjudicated by authority. Local bishops and particular councils often spoke first, with Rome or a general council entering only upon appeal. Popes, when they did intervene, were normally indulgent toward those who were found to be in error. To illustrate this leniency, Newman instances the treatment of Pelagius, Coelestius, and Berengarius.[12]

In a private letter to Frederic Roger, Baron Blachford, of February 5, 1875, Newman explains that the Catholic Church, like Great Britain, has a constitutional form of polity that protects her against the excesses of individuals, whether hierarchical or lay. Just as lawyers and public offices preserve the body politic from the absolutistic tendencies of kings and lords, so, Newman argues, the theological schools (the *schola theologorum*) protect the Church from the encroachments of popes and councils.[13]

In his *Letter to the Duke of Norfolk* Newman shows how the definitive pronouncements of the Church kindle the processes of theological inquiry. Hardly has the Church magisterially declared some doctrine, when she sets her theologians to work to explain its meaning by precise interpretation of the wording, the intention, and the circumstances, and by making room for appropriate exceptions. Theologians will generally strive to keep the doctrine from being unnecessarily burdensome and to diminish the temptation for self-willed, independent, or poorly educated minds to reject it.[14]

'None but the *Schola Theologorum*,' he writes to the Duke of Norfolk, 'is competent to determine the force of Papal and Synodal utterances, and the exact interpretation of them is a matter of time.'[15] In some cases principles that seem to be universal admit of exceptions in their actual application. For example, the doctrine 'Outside the Church no salvation,' Newman observes, seems on the surface to debar all non-Catholics from eternal life; yet theologians explain it as allowing for the salvation of persons who, being invincibly ignorant of the true religion, cooperate as best they can with the light and grace given to them. Another example is the condemnation of usury.[16] The Council of Vienna in the fourteenth century seemed to prohibit the taking of interest altogether, but as a result of theological discussion the prohibition was subsequently interpreted as allowing for the taking of interest in certain cases.[17] With examples such as these, Newman anticipates the thought of Karl Rahner to the effect that every dogmatic proclamation is not only an end but also a beginning.[18] The decision of any one question opens up new questions for the theological schools.

The Church and science

The vexed question of the relationship between revelation and science did not greatly trouble Newman, because to him it seemed evident that revelation does not teach anything about physical science. Ecclesiastical authority and science, he writes, have not thus far fallen into any real conflict because the methods of experimental science are so new that the history of their relations with theology has yet to develop. The Church has kept clear of scientific questions except for the case of Galileo – the exception that proves the rule.[19]

Newman's most thorough treatment of the relationship between theology and the physical sciences is in *The Idea of a University*. In

Discourse IX he denies that there can be any real collision between natural science and Catholicism, because nature and grace, reason and revelation come from the same Author.[20] The Church has no call to enter into scientific questions, but she must defend revelation when science seeks to discredit or adulterate it, or when scientists disseminate unproved theories that are upsetting large segments of the faithful. Newman blames Galileo for not staying within his own province but for going out of his way to insult the received interpretation of Scripture. Theologians quite naturally repelled his wanton and arrogant attack.[21]

In the 'Occasional Lectures' on university subjects, appended to the *Idea of a University*, Newman gives a more penetrating analysis of the relations between Christianity and scientific investigation. Confident though he is that there can be no real collision between theological and scientific truth, he acknowledges that Christian believers, in accordance with the common belief of their contemporaries, interpreted the Bible as teaching that the earth was immovable. If ecclesiastical authorities ever sought to enforce these human traditions to the detriment of scientific investigation, it was a case of undue interference in the province of physics. At least the Church herself never required her members to accept these popular interpretations of Scripture.[22]

Newman admits that certain scientific discoveries may seem at first sight to conflict with Christian faith. He warns religious leaders not to intervene too hastily. Scientists must be allowed to proceed by the methods of their own discipline rather than let their investigations be continually interrupted by objections brought from a higher branch of learning. Like other thinkers, scientists need elbow-room. If they were required to reconcile their hypotheses at every stage of development with all that divines have said and with whatever the multitude have believed about religious matters, they would be paralyzed in their labors, and could accomplish nothing at all.[23] It is not surprising, then, that some outstanding Catholic scientists have incurred occasional criticisms from ecclesiastical authority. The same may be said of some philosophers such as Nicolas de Malebranche and of religious thinkers such as Cardinal Noris, Bossuet, and Muratori. Even if these authors erred on some minor points, 'their services to religion were on the whole far too important to allow of their being molested by critical observation in detail.'[24]

The freedom of theology

Just as Newman championed the liberty of scientists to pursue their own studies unhindered, so likewise he strove to preserve the necessary space for theologians to conduct their speculations without fear of reprisal. In the *Apologia*, after praising the freedom allowed to theologians in the Middle Ages, he adds that such freedom depends upon a certain distance between theology and the supreme magisterium of the Church. The theologian would not dare to propose new theories

> if he knew an authority, which was supreme and final, was watching every word he said, and made signs of assent or dissent to each sentence, as he uttered it. Then indeed he would be fighting, as the Persian soldiers, under the lash, and the freedom of his intellect might truly be said to be beaten out of him. But this has not been so.[25]

Newman as a Catholic found himself constantly engaged in a battle on two fronts. On the one hand, he was confronting liberals and unbelievers who contested the Church's right to teach with authority, and on the other hand, he was anxious to stave off arbitrary and capricious exercises of authority, which, he felt, would play into the hands of the Church's enemies. In the brief dedicatory epistle to the Duke of Norfolk with which he introduces his response to Gladstone's *Expostulation*, Newman candidly admits that in the midst of the present excitement he finds

> knots of Catholics here and there ... who for years past have conducted themselves as if no responsibility attached to wild words and overbearing deeds; who have stated truths in the most paradoxical form, and stretched principles till they were close upon snapping; and who at length, having done their best to set the house on fire, leave to others the task of putting out the flame.[26]

Toward the end of the book, echoing the same theme, he mentions 'that there has been of late years a fierce and intolerant temper abroad, which scorns and virtually tramples on the little ones of Christ.'[27]

Because he counted on the theological schools as a kind of buffer zone, Newman frequently lamented their virtual destruction by the

French Revolution and other recent calamities. In a letter to William Monsell of January 13, 1863 he observes mournfully:

> The wisdom of the Church has provided many courts for theological questions, one higher than another, and with an appeal from the lower to the higher. I suppose, in the middle ages, which has a manliness and boldness of which there is now so great a lack, a question was first debated in a University; then one University against another; or by one order of friars against another; then perhaps it came before a theological faculty; then it went to the metropolitan; and so by various stages and after many examinations and judgments, it came before the Holy See. But now what do the Bishops do? All courts are superseded, because the whole English-speaking population all over the world is under Propaganda, an arbitrary, military power. Propaganda is our only court of appeal, but to it the Bishops go, and secure it and commit it, before they move one step in the matter which calls for interference. And how is Propaganda to know anything about an English controversy, since it talks Italian? by extempore translation (I do not speak at random) or by exparte assertion of some narrowminded Bishop, – narrowminded, though he may be saintly too. And who *is* Propaganda? one sharp man of business, who works day and night, and dispatches his work quick off, to the East and the West, a high dignitary, perhaps an Archbishop, but after all little more than a clerk.[28]

Many of the same themes recur in Newman's passionate letter of May 19, 1863, to Emily Bowles: 'There are no schools now, no private judgment (in the *religious* sense of the phrase), no freedom, that is, of opinion.'[29]

We shall have occasion to return to the dialectical tension between theologians and the ecclesiastical magisterium, but not before we have given some consideration to a third class of persons in the Church – lay persons who are not theologians.

The consultative role of the laity

In 1859 Newman presented some fascinating ideas on the interaction between the episcopate and the laity in an article 'On Consulting the Faithful in Matters of Doctrine,' which he later republished in condensed form as an appendix to his book on *The Arians of the Fourth Century*.[30] This article, as noted in chapter 1 above, got Newman into trouble. The very idea that the hierarchy ought to consult the laity before pronouncing on doctrinal matters was in some quarters considered audacious if not false. Even more unsettling was Newman's assertion that in the Arian crisis the magisterium fell short of its responsibility, so that the true faith was better maintained by the people than by their bishops. His words sounded rather harsh:

> [T]here was a temporary suspense of the functions of the 'Ecclesia docens.' The body of Bishops failed in their confession of the faith. They spoke variously, one against another; there was nothing, after Nicaea, of firm, unvarying, consistent testimony, for nearly sixty years. There were untrustworthy Councils, unfaithful Bishops; there was weakness, fear of consequences, misguidance, delusion, hallucination, endless, hopeless, extending itself into nearly every corner of the Catholic Church. The comparatively few who remained faithful were discredited and driven into exile; the rest were either deceivers or were deceived.[31]

Newman follows this paragraph with some ten pages of supporting evidence from many sectors of the early Church, including a quotation from St. Hilary declaring that 'the ears of the people are holier than the hearts of the bishops.'[32] It is for historians to judge whether Newman went beyond the evidence.[33] He may have been misled by relying too much on lay historians who were unfriendly to the bishops.[34]

For our purposes, the main interest of Newman's essay consists in what it says about the prior consensus or subsequent reception by the faithful as criteria for teaching. The great body of the faithful, according to Newman, reject false teaching when it is proposed to them because they have within them a principle of orthodoxy. Even though not schooled in scientific theology, they have an infused sense of the true faith thanks to the Holy Spirit who dwells with his gifts and graces in the entire Church. Newman speaks of a kind of Christian instinct or tact implanted in the faithful by the Holy Spirit, by reason of which they are impelled to accept authentic teaching and reject heresy. This instinct, deeply implanted in the bosom of the mystical Body of Christ, lies at the root of the supernatural illative sense discussed above in Chapter 3. With a reference to the German theologian Johann Adam Möhler, Newman maintained as early as 1850 that nations are governed by a vital spirit in matters of religion:

We know that it is a property of life to be impatient of any foreign substance in the body to which it belongs. It will be sovereign in its own domain, and it conflicts with what it cannot assimilate into itself, and *is irritated and disordered* till it has expelled it. Such expulsion, then, is emphatically a test of uncongeniality, for it shows that the substance ejected, not only is not one with the body that rejects it, but cannot be made one with it; that its introduction is not only useless, or superfluous, or adventitious, but that it is intolerable.[35]

In his essay *On Consulting the Faithful* Newman quotes this paragraph and yet another passage from the same work:

The religious life of a people is of a certain quality and direction, and these are tested by the mode in which it encounters the various opinions, customs, and institutions which are submitted to it. Drive a stake into a river's bed, and you will at once ascertain which way it is running, and at what speed; throw up even a straw into the air, and you will see which way the wind blows; submit your heretical and Catholic principle to the action of the multitude, and you will be able to pronounce at once whether it is imbued with Catholic truth or with heretical falsehood.[36]

To confirm the orthodoxy of his position Newman points out that Pope Pius IX took soundings to ascertain the sentiments of the faithful before defining the doctrine of the Immaculate Conception in 1854. In his Encyclical *Ubi primum* of 1849 the Holy Father asked the bishops of the whole Catholic world to inform him whether the clergy and faithful of their dioceses believed that Mary had been sinless from the moment of her conception and that her freedom from original sin was a revealed truth that should be defined. The answers to both questions were overwhelmingly positive, so that in the bull of definition the pope could refer to the remarkable consensus (*singularis conspiratio*) of the Catholic bishops and faithful as one ground for the definition.[37]

Newman therefore regarded the laity, constituting the great majority of the faithful people of God, as having a certain competence not only in matters of devotion but also in doctrine. To be framers and judges of ecclesiastical doctrine was indeed the prerogative of popes and bishops. The laity normally echoed in their beliefs what the pastors had taught them.[38] Thus their competence in doctrine, as Newman saw it, was chiefly indirect. While not themselves making doctrinal proposals or pronounce-ments, they were qualified to discern the difference between doctrines that were harmonious with their faith and those opposed to it.

Newman sometimes distinguished between the infallibility of the whole Church in believing and that of the magisterium, as a part of the Church, in teaching. Without maintaining that the laity were by themselves infallible in matters of doctrine, he considered their united testimony to be a reliable indication of the faith of the entire Church, which was infallible. Newman's views, controversial in his own day, were vindicated by Vatican II, especially in its Constitution on the Church, which speaks of the supernatural sense of the faith that inheres in the whole people of God, thanks to the Spirit of truth.[39] The universal body of the faithful, according to the Council, cannot be mistaken when it expresses beliefs held by the consensus of all the faithful, including both clergy and laity.

The testimony of the laity, Newman observed, was of particular value in doctrinal matters that had a direct bearing upon devotional sentiments. As examples he gave not only the Immaculate Concep-tion, but also the divinity of Christ, the doctrine of the Real Presence, and the blessedness of the saints in heaven. With abundant allusions to history, Newman showed how the sense of the faithful had influenced all four of these doctrines. He concludes his essay with a fifth example: the enthusiasm of the people of Ephesus on the occasion of the definition of Mary's title as Mother of God.[40]

The laity and theology

Newman, writing within the horizons of his own day, considered it rather exceptional for lay people to be theologians. In his Catholic University at Dublin he fought hard against some of the Irish prelates to obtain lay professors for chairs in non-theological disciplines but he expected the faculty of theology to consist of priests. The lay students, however, were to receive a solid training in theology.

Although Newman did not see dogmatic theology as a common vocation of the laity, he looked forward to the formation of a class of mature Christians with a keen sense of the faith. Assuming that lay persons would ordinarily be engaged in secular pursuits, he expected them to bear witness to the gospel in their homes, their social contacts, and their places of work. They should accordingly obtain a theological training that would equip them to answer questions that would be likely to arise in their social and occupational activities.[41]

In his lectures on *The Idea of a University* Newman notes that while the laity in the past rarely distinguished themselves as dogmatic theologians, analyzing the faith from within, many of them have shown great ability in delineating the faith from without, as it appears to people mixing in the world. The most successful lay theologians, he observed, have been apologists such as, in the first age, Justin, Athenagoras, Arnobius, and Lactantius, or in the nineteenth century, Joseph de Maistre, François René de Chateaubriand, Auguste Nicolas, and Charles de Montalembert.[42]

Newman's position on lay theology is well summarized at the conclusion of his work on *The Present Position of Catholics in England*:

> I want a laity, not arrogant, not rash in speech, not disputatious, but men who know their religion, who enter into it, who know just where they stand, who know what they hold, and what they do not, who know their creed so well, that they can give an account of it, who know so much of history that they can defend it.[43]

A century after Newman, Yves Congar, building to some degree on Newman's work, expressed the desire that lay people should personally appropriate the Catholic tradition and pass it on by faithfully living it. He maintained that the laity may have charisms of knowledge, as did the two Teresas, Pascal, and others, although they cannot teach with authority in their own right. Their competence is especially in the realms of private exhortation or admonition. By echoing the voice of apostolic authority, they can corroborate it. Like Newman, Congar remarks on the multitude of apologists who have been laymen, mentioning many of the same names. But the realm of dogmatic theology, according to Congar, is normally reserved to priests, because such theology is intimately related to the sacraments, ecclesiastical tradition, and pastoral care.[44] Congar does not claim the authority of Newman for these further specifications, but Newman, I suspect, would agree with them.

The threefold office

Toward the end of his life, in 1877, Newman brought the roles of the hierarchy, the theologians, and the laity into a brilliant synthesis in the Preface to the third edition of his *Via Media*.[45] Reviewing the text of his work on the prophetical office, he finds in it two main charges against the Roman Catholic Church: that modern Catholicism departs from primitive Christianity and that its popular and political manifestations differ from its formal teaching. The first charge, he feels, has been sufficiently answered in his *Essay on Development*. Now he wishes to address the second.[46]

Newman depicts the Church as possessing three essential powers or functions, which he connects rather imprecisely with the offices of Christ as priest, prophet, and king. As a worshiping community, the Church is priestly. As a community of thought and education, it is prophetic. As an organized society equipped with governing functions, it is regal.[47]

From the beginning, Newman says, all three functions were exercised in the Church, but they achieved their maturity in succession. In the first centuries the Church appeared principally as a community of worship. Worship led naturally to confession and, on occasion, to heroic acts of martyrdom. In the next few centuries a class of cultivated intellectuals emerged, creating schools of learning. Finally, the Church developed a well-established ecclesiastical polity under the hegemony of the bishop of Rome.[48]

These three functions of the Church, according to Newman, are not really separable. None of them operates except by interaction with the other two. The health and growth of the Church result from cooperation and creative tension among all three functions. Popular religion is the broad base that gives vitality to the whole organism. Theological reflection gives clarity and identifies aberrations. Ecclesiastical authority coordinates the life and doctrine of the Church. It prevents the excesses of popular piety and the extremes of critical thought from relapsing into pagan superstitions or misrepresenting the Church's faith.[49]

The different functions of the Church, Newman holds, arise out of different concerns, all legitimate. 'Truth is the guiding principle of theology and theological inquiries; devotion and edification, of worship; and of government, expedience.'[50] The three use different means. 'The instrument of theology is reasoning; of worship, our emotional nature; of rule, command and coercion.'[51] Then again, the three are liable to different corruptions. Reasoning tends to rationalism and skepticism; devotion, to superstition and enthusiasm; and power, to ambition and tyranny.[52]

Newman thus sets up a fascinating dialectic within the Church.

The three powers – priestly, prophetic, and regal – are mutually complementary. No one of them is unequivocally superior to the other two. The laity and the pastors embody, on the whole, the devotional principle; the theologians, the rational; and the papacy and its curia, the regiminal.[53] It is normal for there to be a certain tension among the three. Popular devotion is impatient with theology for being too critical and academic, and with the hierarchy for being too political and authoritarian. Theologians bristle at the exuberance of popular piety and chafe at the restraints imposed upon them by the hierarchy. The hierarchy are on guard against the credulity of uneducated believers and the rationalism of theologians.

Notwithstanding the tensions, each office is partly dependent on the other two. Without the reverence of simple piety neither the theologians nor the ecclesiastical magisterium could sustain a living communion with the Object of the Church's faith. Popular devotions, however, are kept within the bounds of orthodoxy by the critical scrutiny of theologians and the vigilance of hierarchical authorities. The magisterium is indebted to theologians for its principles, concepts, and technical vocabulary. The theologians depend on the guidance of the magisterium to provide secure grounding for their speculations.

Newman therefore develops an ecclesiology of checks and balances. Without minimizing the pastoral authority of hierarchical leaders, he proposes a complex system that is evidently indebted not only to biblical authors such as Paul but also to the British political experience. Although the Church is, from one point of view, a structured hierarchical society, it is also a people whose members vitally interact. All the members of the Church, whether lay or clerical, whether simple believers or learned theologians, must learn from one another and be solicitous for the good of the entire organism.

By referring to this interplay of offices and concerns, Newman answers some of the charges made in *The Prophetical Office*. That book was unjust, he says, in charging the schoolmen with ambition, insincerity, craft, and cruelty. Theology has on the whole restrained and corrected these deviations, and could do so even more effectively had the schools of theology not been broken up.[54] Popular devotion does tend toward excesses in the cult of the saints, relics, and images, but superstition, Newman says, is not the worst of evils. Often enough, it is the shadow side of a living popular faith.[55] The regal office, far from being overbearing, has generally acted with great moderation in tolerating deviations rather than quench the smoking flax or uproot the good grain with the chaff.[56]

Newman's treatment of the three offices is highly original. It differs markedly from the continental tradition of Catholic theology and canon law, exemplified by authors such as Ferdinand Walter, George Phillips, Heinrich Klee, Johann Baptist Franzelin, Clemens Schrader, and Joseph Kleutgen – authors whose works Newman probably never read. Like Newman, these authors distinguish the offices of sanctifying, ruling, and teaching, but unlike him they ascribe all three offices in their fullness to the pope and bishops. After Newman, Friedrich von Hügel proposed a philosophy of religion in which the institutional, rational, and mystical elements dialectically interact, but he did not develop this theme ecclesiologically.[57] Even Vatican II, which sees all members of the Church as participating in all three offices, emphasizes only the harmony, not the tension.

Newman, therefore, was a pioneer in pointing out that the demands of worship, academic study, and ecclesiastical expediency stand in tension, and that the various elements in the Church exercise a healthy restraining influence upon one another. His schematization has certain weaknesses, inasmuch as it seems to suggest that the pope and his curia are motivated chiefly by expediency, that truth is the special preserve of theologians, and that priesthood is primarily exercised by the laity. But he is correct in pointing out the diversity of functions and the need for mutual understanding and, at times, for compromise. The hierarchical leaders may have to refrain from condemning relatively innocuous doctrinal deviations so that the theological community may enjoy a proper freedom and autonomy, relying on its own self-corrective mechanisms. At times, too, theologians and bishops should tolerate theologically unwarranted popular devotions rather than crush a lively and heartfelt faith. Theologians and lay persons, likewise, must respect the special responsibilities of the hierarchy to maintain unity and continuity, and refrain from hastily accusing them of abusing their powers. If Newman's realism were put into practice, the Church might be spared some of the bitter controversies that have recently arisen over questions such as the ordination of women and the supervision of liturgical translations.

It is remarkable that Newman, eager as he was to defend the authority of apostolic office and the infallibility of the magisterium, would also champion so energetically the rights of theologians and lay persons. The archenemy of liberalism, he was also champion of liberty. Insistent though he was on the prerogatives of authority, he was ever on guard against its abuses. Newman's thought was complex and many-faceted. His writings on the freedom of theology and on the active role of the laity in the Church make it difficult to speak of him as authoritarian. Those who quote him as seeming to favor the hierarchy over the laity or pastoral office over theology must speak with great caution. Their adversaries may come up with a quotation from Newman that seems to favor the opposite point of view. Newman cannot be studied through excerpts, but only by a grasp of his thinking in its full range.

Notes

1   Newman, *Certain Difficulties Felt by Anglicans in Catholic Teaching Considered*, 2 vols. (London: Longmans, Green & Co., 1908, 1910), vol. 1, p. 128, hereafter abbreviated *Diff*.

2   Ibid., p. 251.

3   Ibid., p. 44.

4   Ibid., p. 247.

5   Newman, *An Essay on the Development of Christian Doctrine* (Notre Dame, IN: University of Notre Dame, 1989), p. 325.

6   Ibid., p. 337.

7   Ibid., p. 338.

8   Newman, *Apologia pro Vita Sua* (London: Longmans, Green & Co., 1929), p. 251; hereafter abbreviated *Apol*.

9   Ibid., p. 252.

10   Ibid., p. 264.

11   Ibid., p. 266.

12   Ibid., p. 268.

13   Newman, *The Letters and Diaries of John Henry Newman* (London: Nelson, 1961–72 Oxford: Clarendon, 1977–), vol. 27, p. 211–13; hereafter abbreviated *LD*.

14   *Diff.*, vol. 2, p. 321.

15   Ibid., p. 176; cf. p. 333.

16   Ibid., pp. 334–6.

17   Ibid., p. 337.

18   Karl Rahner, 'Current Problems in Christology,' in his *Theological Investigations* 1 (Baltimore: Helicon, 1961), pp. 149–200, at p. 150.

19 *Apol.*, p. 264.

20 Newman, *The Idea of a University Defined and Illustrated*, ed. I. T. Ker (Oxford: Clarendon, 1976), p. 219. For the sake of convenience, I use the page references to the uniform edition of Newman's works, which Ker prints in the margins; hereafter abbreviated *Idea*.

21 Ibid., p. 220.

22 Ibid., pp. 443–4.

23 Ibid., pp. 475–6.

24 Ibid., p. 478.

25 *Apol.*, pp. 267–8.

26 *Diff.*, vol. 2, pp. 176–7.

27 Ibid., p. 339.

28 *LD*, vol. 20, p. 391.

29 *LD* vol. 20, p. 447.

30 Newman, *On Consulting the Faithful in Matters of Doctrine.* The version edited by John Coulson (Kansas City, Missouri, Sheed & Ward, 1985) reproduces on pp. 53–106 the full text from *The Rambler* 1 (new series, part II, July 1859), pp. 198–230. Coulson also gives on pp. 109–118 the condensed and modified form of the article published by Newman as an Appendix to *The Arians of the Fourth Century*, third ed., 1871. I shall follow the pagination in the Coulson edition; hereafter abbreviated *CF*.

31 *CF*, p. 77.

32 Ibid., p. 85, quoting Hilary of Poitiers, *In Auxentium*, § 6.

33 Michael Slusser, 'Does Newman's 'On Consulting the Faithful in Matters of Doctrine' Rest upon a Mistake?' *Horizons* 20 (1993), pp. 234–40. In agreement with the Protestant patrologist R. P. C. Hanson he concludes: 'We should dismiss the 'romantic suggestion' that the ordinary faithful as a body clung to Nicene orthodoxy despite the vacillation of their bishops' (p. 239).

34 Yves Congar in *Lay People in the Church* (Westminster, MD: Newman, 1957), p. 273 speaks of Newman's excessive reliance on Socrates and Sozomen. Jules Lebreton, according to Congar, 'puts the break not between the faithful and the hierarchy but between the people's faith and the risky speculations of theologians,' ibid., n. 13.

35 *Diff.*, vol.1, pp. 52–3.

36 *CF*, pp. 74–5; cf. *Diff.*, vol. 1, p. 55.

37 *CF*, p. 71.

38 Ibid., pp. 72 and 103.

39 Vatican II, Dogmatic Constitution on the Church, *Lumen gentium*, p. 12.

40   *CF*, pp. 104–5.

41   *Idea*, pp. 377–8.

42   Ibid., p. 379.

43   Newman, *Lectures on the Present Position of Catholics in England* (New York: America Press, 1942), p. 300.

44   Congar, *Lay People*, pp. 278–97.

45   Newman, *Via Media* 1 (London: Longmans, Green & Co., 1891), pp. xv–xciv; hereafter abbreviated *VM*. I shall indicate the pages according to the Latin numbers given to them in Newman's Preface. Concerning the Preface see Avery Dulles, 'The Threefold Office in Newman's Ecclesiology,' in *Newman after a Hundred Years*, ed. Ian Ker and Alan G. Hill (Oxford: Clarendon Press, 1990), pp. 275–99.

46   *VM*, vol. 1, pp. xxxvii–xxxviii.

47   Ibid., p. xl.

48   Ibid., pp. xl and xli.

49   Ibid., pp. xlvi–xlvii.

50   Ibid., p. xli.

51   Ibid.

52   Ibid.

53   Ibid., p. xl.

54   Ibid., p. xlvii.

55   Ibid., p. lxix.

56   Ibid., pp. lx, lxv.

57   Friedrich von Hügel, *The Mystical Element of Religion as Studied in Saint Catherine of Genoa an Her Friends*, 2 vols. (2nd ed., London: J. M. Dent, 1911), vol. 1, pp. 50–82.

8

The Church and the Churches

The one true Church

As Newman found his way toward the Roman Catholic communion he abandoned the Branch Theory, according to which the
Catholic Church was made up of several distinct communions,
which Newman named as the Greek, the Roman, and the Anglican.
He became convinced that the Roman communion alone was the
true and Catholic Church, and that all bodies not in union with
Rome were schismatical or heretical.[1]

When he launched his Catholic apostolate in England, after
returning from his studies in Rome, Newman triumphantly asserted
the exclusive prerogatives of the Catholic Church. 'It is my intimate
sense,' he wrote, 'that the Catholic Church is the one ark of
salvation' and 'that Church in which alone is salvation.'[2] In his
letters he refers to it as 'the only true Church,'[3] and the 'One Fold of
Christ.'[4] We have the conviction, he wrote, 'that the Catholic
religion is given from God for the salvation of mankind, and that
all other religions are but mockeries.'[5]

The true Church, for Newman, must necessarily be a single
communion and could not contain elements that were 'independent
of the whole, discordant with one another in doctrine and in ritual,
destitute of mutual intercommunion, and more frequently in actual
warfare, portion with portion, than in a state of neutrality.'[6] How
could the true Church, he asked, include a 'Russian Branch, which
denounces the Pope as a usurper,' and a 'Papal, which

anathematizes the Protestantism of the Anglican,' not to mention other forms of Christianity which reject the real presence of Christ in the Eucharist and even put aside the Athanasian creed?[7]

Newman did not hesitate to employ his literary talents in defense of the Catholic Church. An occasion arose in 1850 with the re-establishment of the Catholic hierarchy in England and the elevation of Nicholas Wiseman to the cardinalate. In the outburst of 'No Popery' that followed, the London Oratorians were burnt in effigy and efforts were made to revive old anti-Catholic legislation. In the following year Newman delivered the nine lectures subsequently collected under the title, *The Present Position of Catholics in England*. The volume is Newman's most brilliant display of his talents as a controversialist. He employs a vast panoply of rhetorical devices, including ridicule and satire. Particularly amusing is the section in which he depicts a group of Russians denouncing ways in which the British apply divine attributes to their monarchy. An imaginary speaker demonstrates that Queen Victoria bears the number of the beast of the Apocalypse, since she was eighteen when she succeeded to the monarchy in 1837. The multiple of eighteen and thirty-seven, he notes, is 666, the number of the beast![8] This book, which Newman considered the best written of all his works, contains comparatively little of theological interest that cannot be better studied in his other works, especially those dealing with contemporary Christianity outside the Catholic Church.

Greece, Russia, and Turkey

When Newman speaks of the Greek communion, he usually includes both the Byzantine (more commonly called the Greek) and the Russian churches.[9] He admits that these churches have true sacraments, a valid sacrifice of the Mass, and authentic priestly orders.[10] But the priests and the flock of that communion are, in his estimation, merely passive believers. Their religion has become mechanical and superstitious.[11] Since both the Byzantine and the Russian churches are merely local or national, their existence, for Newman, poses no serious objection against the catholicity of the Roman communion, which alone is independent of all geographical and political limitations.[12] Newman dismisses the long period of separation from the West as being for these churches 'eight centuries ... of religious deadness and insensibility.'[13] Yet he rallies to the defense of Russia in the Crimean War. When England

and France supported Turkey against Russia, he protests that they should be taking the side of the Czar, as a Christian monarch is 'attacking an infamous Power, the enemy of God and man.'[14] 'Since the year 1048,' he declares, Muslim Turkey has been 'the great Antichrist among the races of men.'[15]

Newman's condemnations of Islam are unsparing. He refers to it as an 'Arabian imposture' and a scourge of God. But he is relieved to note that it is 'only an indigenous religion, and that in certain portions of two continents, with little power or wish to propagate its faith.'[16] It would be hard today to defend Newman's assessment of Islam as a torpid and moribund religion. He manifestly failed to anticipate the recrudescence of Islamic faith and missionary expansion in the twentieth century.

Vestiges of Catholicism

Regarding the Protestant and Anglican churches as cut off from the true communion, Newman was disposed to reject their sacraments and ministries. He was doubtful – and increasingly doubtful as the years passed – about the validity of Anglican ordinations. In a letter of July 30, 1857 to Ambrose Phillipps de Lisle, he takes the irreverence of the Anglican clergy toward the Blessed Sacrament as indirect evidence that they do not validly consecrate.[17] Writing to Edward Husband on July 17, 1870, Newman remarks that when he became a Catholic in 1845 he did not yet have 'that utter distrust of the Anglican Orders which I feel in 1870.'[18] The fact that Anglicans experience peace and joy of soul when receiving their sacraments proves nothing to the contrary, for these sentiments may well be due to the personal devotion of the recipients rather than to the efficacy of the sacramental rite itself.[19]

Newman did not, however, deny the likelihood that Anglicans would receive visitations of God's grace. When he began to question the apostolic character of Anglican orders and sacraments, he still considered that Church to be a part of God's people. He compared dissident churches to the Ten Tribes after they had been separated from the kingdom of David and the Aaronic priesthood. Just as God had sent prophets such as Elijah and Elisha to the schismatic Israelites, so he might raise up holy ministers among Protestants and Anglicans.[20] Later, as a Catholic, he judged the analogy with the Northern Kingdom to be misleading, but he continued to believe that Christians in separation from Rome might expect to receive God's uncovenanted mercies.

In a letter of April 26, 1841, toward the end of his Anglican period, he wrote to the Catholic theologian Charles W. Russell that the long duration of Protestantism was evidence that it must contain many and great truths, for so much piety and earnestness must be rooted in a measure of truth.[21] As a Catholic, Newman admitted without hesitation that Protestants and Anglicans have a valid baptism and have retained some scattered fragments of that 'large floating body of Catholic truth' that had been poured into all quarters of the globe, while being found 'in fulness and purity in the [Catholic] Church alone.'[22] He dared to hope that the Bible and the Anglican Prayer Book retain enough Catholic truth for many Protestants, separated from the true Church in good faith, to be saved.[23] In one of his last letters he testified that he continued to cherish 'those great and burning truths' that he had learned from Calvinist Evangelicals as a boy.[24] Nevertheless he denied that he owed anything religiously to Protestantism, for he held that the doctrines of the Holy Trinity, the Incarnation, grace, election, good works, and divine life in the soul, which he had imbibed from Evangelical authors such as Thomas Scott, were not specific to Protestantism but were parts of the Catholic legacy that had come down from Christian antiquity.

As a Catholic, therefore, Newman denies that Anglicans can receive grace as a gift of their own Church. Some of his statements seem unduly harsh. The Church of England, he once wrote, was nothing but 'a tomb of what was once living, the casket of a treasure which has been lost.'[25] Anglicans, he declared, could no more receive grace from their own church than 'an infant could receive nourishment from the breast of its dead mother.'[26] Whatever grace they did receive came through the Catholic Church, part of whose patrimony had been preserved in Anglicanism.

The faith of Protestants

Newman as a Catholic often expressed uncertainty about whether Protestants really had the virtue of faith. In *Loss and Gain* the hero, Charles Reding, discusses this question with a priest, who probably speaks for Newman himself. Reding declares that he has many acquaintances who

> from knowledge of the Gospels, have an absolute conviction and an intimate sense of the reality of the sacred facts contained in

them, which, whether you call it faith or not, is powerful enough to colour their whole being with its influence, and rules their heart and conduct as well as their imagination. I can't believe that these persons are out of God's favour.[27]

The priest replies that if Protestants really believe these things on the authority of Scripture, and are inculpably ignorant of the biblical teachings they reject, they may have faith. It is possible that they receive the Scriptures as divinely authoritative on the word of the Church. But he fears that 'taking the nation as a whole, there are few who on this score can lay claim to faith.'[28]

In his *Discourses to Mixed Congregations* Newman devotes many pages to the faith of non-Catholics. He admits that many of them accept truths that belong to the deposit of Christian faith, but he has questions about the motives on which they believe. Perhaps, he says, they are simply repeating doctrines that were taught to them in childhood, rather than affirming them with personal conviction. Perhaps they are attracted to the beauty of Christian doctrines and rites but have never put to themselves the hard question of truth. Or perhaps, again, the Protestant is merely speculating about what might be true, without firmly assenting to it on the authority of revelation. Although Protestants seem to adhere to some revealed truths, their rejection of other revealed truths indicates that they do not have the vision of faith.[29] Some Protestants, according to Newman, actually consider it a fault to be certain about matters of faith and a merit to doubt.[30]

Newman then goes on to explain that having faith, in the Catholic sense, means firmly assenting to a doctrine as true because God teaches it through an accredited messenger. In apostolic times the gospel was received on the word of the apostles, which was taken as the word of God. To believe in the word of a living authority is quite different from taking a book in one's hands and interpreting it for oneself. Protestants, when they profess to believe the Bible, reserve the right to explain it for themselves. For this reason they do not have faith in the sense that it was exercised by the first Christians. 'In the Apostles' days the peculiarity of faith was submission to a living authority. If you will not look out for a living authority, and will bargain for private judgment, then say at once that you have not Apostolic faith.'[31]

Carrying his argument one stage further, Newman proceeds to connect faith with infallibility. The Established Church, he says, cannot exact faith from its members because it is not infallible. Its members commonly adhere to it because they cherish the religion in which they were brought up or because they are attracted to its decency and order or the cadenced prose of its Prayer Book, rather than because they are submitting to its teaching as divine revelation. 'Nothing is clearer than this, that if faith in God's word is required of us for salvation, the Catholic Church is the only medium by which we can exercise it.'[32]

In his lectures on Anglican Difficulties, delivered the following year (1850), Newman somewhat tempers the severe conclusions of his *Discourses to Mixed Congregations.* In principle, he says, members of heretical and schismatical churches are always in danger of falling into a merely material faith – that is to say, habitual belief based on what is familiar to them from their family and culture. But he notes that many members of these communities were validly baptized as infants, and that God's grace may be impelling them to seek the fullness of God's revelation.[33] Thus there may be exceptions to the rule that they cannot have faith. The more exceptions there are, the more is God to be praised! The anti-Catholicism of religious or civic leaders does not suffice to destroy the heritage of revealed truth and worship that comes down from Christian antiquity. 'There may be many ... who, being in invincible ignorance on those particular points of religion on which their Communion is wrong, may still have the divine and unclouded illumination of faith on those numerous points on which it is right.'[34] We may reasonably hope, therefore, that vast multitudes in Greece, in Russia, and in England are in a state of good faith and are on the way to salvation. Even Protestants who have received no sacrament since they were baptized in infancy may, through God's grace, find in the written Word of God the divine instrument of bringing them to contrition and to a happy death.[35]

These possible exceptions, however, should not be turned into excuses for those whose ignorance is vincible or who actually know that their own communion is in schism or heresy. Those who receive the grace to recognize the unique claims of the Catholic Church have a duty to act. If they do not act upon the knowledge granted to them, they are in serious danger of losing their souls.[36]

The Anglican establishment

Newman's ambivalent attitude toward the Church of England becomes dramatically manifest in a series of statements he made over the years about the establishment of Anglicanism as the national religion.

In the *Difficulties of Anglicans*, a set of lectures directed primarily to his former associates in the Oxford Movement, Newman argued that they should follow him in submitting to Rome. The Established Religion of England, he contended, was irretrievably Erastian. The English Church was completely subject to the civil power; its bishops and parochial clergy were officers of the State.[37] 'It has no traditions; it cannot be said to think; it does not know what it holds, and what it does not. ... [I]ts Prayer-Book is an Act of Parliament of two centuries ago, and its cathedrals and chapter-houses are the spoils of Catholicism.'[38]

Newman was quite aware that some high churchmen were reluctant to submit to Rome because they felt obliged to work from within for the catholicity of the Anglican communion, which they regarded as the Church of their baptism. They were tempted to feel that by remaining where they were, they could influence the Anglican communion to become more Catholic.

Seeking to disabuse these Anglo-Catholics, Newman contends that the Oxford Movement, with its aim to emancipate the Church from subjection to the Crown and to rid it of its Protestant elements, is engaged in a hopeless task. The national State, which has an iron grip on the Church, will never tolerate double jurisdiction or divided allegiance. The State could not recognize any rival authority without weakening its own.[39] The Church of England, as a creature of the State, could never become truly catholic or apostolic. For all these reasons Newman pleads with Anglo-Catholics to abandon the Church of England and come over to Rome. England could not be made Catholic from within the Church of England, but only from outside, by a mission from the Catholic Church.[40] 'You can have no trust in the Establishment or its Sacraments and ordinances. You must leave it, you must secede.'[41]

But this brief against the Establishment does not represent the full thrust of Newman's thought. He makes many positive statements about the value of the State religion. In three letters written in late 1850 and early 1851 to the Catholic layman J. M. Capes, Newman warned him against launching a crusade against the Establishment. Newman here depicted the Church of England as 'a bulwark against infidelity,' in the shadow of which all the dissenting churches lived. While the Established Church survived, Newman believed, it served as a witness to revelation and to dogmatical and ritual religion. If the Anglican Establishment were overthrown, infidel literature would, so to speak, flood the market. The Catholic Church was not yet strong enough to take the place of the Establishment in this regard.[42]

In 1860 Newman declined to take part in plans to build a new Catholic church at Oxford, on the ground that it might diminish the influence of Anglicanism there. In a letter to Bishop Ullathorne's secretary, Canon E. E. Estcourt, he explained his reasons at some length:

> While I do not see my way to take steps to weaken the Church of England, being what it is, least of all should I be disposed to do so in Oxford, which has hitherto been the seat of those traditions which constitute whatever there is of Catholic doctrine and principle in the Anglican Church. ... Till things are very much changed there, in weakening Oxford, we are weakening our friends, weakening our own *de facto* παιδαγωγός into the Church. Catholics did not make us Catholics, Oxford made us Catholics. At present Oxford surely does more good than harm. ...
>
> I go further than mere tolerance at Oxford; as I have said, I wish to suffer the Church of England. The Establishment has ever been a breakwater against Unitarianism, fanaticism, and infidelity. It has ever loved us better than Puritans and Independents have loved us. ... And it receives all that abuse and odium of dogmatism, or at least a good deal of it, which otherwise would be directed against us.[43]

In subsequent years Newman maintained approximately the same position. In a letter of June 7, 1863, to his Anglican friend Isaac Williams, he wrote: 'The Anglican Church has been a most useful breakwater against scepticism,' but in the same letter he expressed his fears that latitudinarian opinions were spreading furiously in the Church of England.[44]

In his *Apologia*, published the following year, Newman recalled his long-standing 'firm belief that grace was to be found within the Anglican Church,'[45] and he added an appendix on 'The Anglican Church' in which he called it 'to a certain point, a witness and teacher of religious truth.'[46] In an autobiographical vein he continued: 'The Church of England has been the instrument of Providence in conferring great benefits on me.' And he added: 'While Catholics are so weak in England, it is doing our work. ...

Doubtless the National Church has hitherto been a serviceable breakwater against doctrinal errors, more fundamental than its own.' For all these reasons he wished to avoid anything that 'went to weaken its hold upon the public mind, or to unsettle its establishment, or to embarrass and lessen its maintenance of those great Christian and Catholic principles and doctrines which it has up to this time successfully preached.'[47]

In a letter of November 1, 1864, to an unknown addressee Newman observed:

> With a violent hand the State kept down the multitude of sects which were laying England waste during the Commonwealth. The State kept out Unitarianism, not to say infidelity, at the era of the Revolution. ... It was the State which prevented the religious enthusiasm of the Methodist revival from destroying dogma. At this moment, destroy the establishment of Anglicanism, and the consequences would be terrible.[48]

Here Newman might have left the matter except that Edward Pusey, in his *Eirenicon*, paraphrased Newman as holding that the Church of England was 'the great bulwark against infidelity in this land.' Cardinal Manning, in a response to Pusey, rejected this appraisal. In his book-length *Letter to Pusey* of 1865, Newman felt obliged to deny that he had ever deliberately called the Anglican Church a bulwark; he repeated from the *Apologia* that he viewed it as 'a serviceable *breakwater* against errors more fundamental than its own.' Unlike a bulwark, he explained, a breakwater is not an integral part of what it defends, and is serviceable if, without excluding error altogether, it detracts from the volume and force of error.[49]

The alternatives of Atheism and Catholicity

As a convert, Newman had to ask himself whether he could make a definitive commitment to his new faith. This raised for him the further question whether certitude in matters of religion was irreversible. In numerous publications he took the position that religious certitudes are, at least normally, irreversible.

We have already seen that Newman as a Catholic continued to affirm what he had previously believed as an Anglican Evangelical. He also retained the convictions he later acquired regarding the existence of the visible Church, the sacramental system, and the dogmatic decrees of the early councils. His conversion, therefore, was not a repudiation but an affirmation and completion of his past; it was continuous, progressive, and incremental.

It seems fair to say that Newman experienced in himself something analogous to the cumulative process he attributed to the whole Church in his *Essay on the Development of Christian Doctrine*. He began, as did the Church in its infancy, with a indistinct global idea not yet articulated in dogmatic statements. In boarding school and at Trinity College he came to accept the great Trinitarian and christological doctrines that were common to all major Christian denominations; then in his years as a tutor at Oriel he perceived the major ecclesiological and sacramental implications, until at length he came to embrace the doctrines specific to Roman Catholicism. His earlier beliefs prepared the way for his later beliefs.

Already as an Anglican, in the last of his Oxford University Sermons (1843), Newman held that the Catholic idea is one and that it implicitly contains all the dogmas. 'These propositions imply each other, as being parts of one whole; so that to deny one is to deny all, and to invalidate one is to deface and destroy the view itself.'[50]

In successive writings Newman spoke of the stages by which an individual comes to a fuller appreciation of the contents of the faith. In his *Discourses to Mixed Congregations* he taught that

> once a man has a real hold of the great doctrine that there is a God, in its true meaning and bearings, then (provided that is no disturbing cause, no peculiarities in his circumstances, involuntary ignorance, or the like), he will be led on without an effort, as by a natural continuation of that belief, to believe also in the Catholic Church as God's Messenger or Prophet ... [51]

In the *Grammar of Assent* (1870), Newman considers whether changes in religious allegiance disprove his thesis that religious certitudes are indefectible. In this connection he briefly analyzes the steps by which a sincere Protestant might find his way to Catholicism. Anyone who assents to the doctrine of our Lord's divinity with a real assent, he concludes, is easily led to welcome the Catholic doctrines of the Real Presence and of Mary as Mother of God (*theotokos*).[52] This hypothetical convert, while making substantial additions to his previous beliefs, has surrendered no conviction that he formerly possessed.

Ten years later, in a new edition of the *Grammar of Assent*,

Newman added an endnote explaining that the first principles, sentiments, and tastes that incline one to accept any revealed truth constitute an *organum investigandi* leading the mind by an infallible succession from the rejection of atheism to monotheism, from monotheism to Christianity, from Christianity to Evangelical religion, and from there to Catholicity.[53]

Corresponding to this theory of an ascending logic leading from theism to Christianity, Newman postulated a descending movement. The disposition that inclines a person to doubt or reject any revealed truth will, if consistently pursued, terminate in total infidelity. In his *Discourses to Mixed Congregations* he argued that when a person ceases to believe in the Church, there is 'nothing in reason to keep him from doubting the existence of God.'[54] 'Unlearn Catholicism,' he wrote, 'and you open the way to your becoming a Protestant, Unitarian, Deist, Pantheist, Sceptic, in a dreadful but inevitable succession.'[55] Already in 1845 Newman had read the autobiography of Blanco White, an Oxford friend who had forsaken the Catholicism of his youth and had ended up as a pantheist.[56]

In the *Apologia* (1864) Newman gives a very succinct summary of his two-edged principle. He reports that by 1844 he had come to the conclusion 'that there was no medium, in true philosophy, between Atheism and Catholicity, and that a perfectly consistent mind, under those circumstances in which it finds itself here below, must embrace either the one or the other.'[57]

This double principle is perhaps Newman's most seminal contribution to ecumenical theology. Although it might seem to suggest that only Catholics have the virtue of faith, it implies rather that all believers, no matter how deficient their professed faith, are secretly reaching forward to the fullness that is professed in Catholic Christianity.

Non-Catholics, to be sure, could hardly be expected to agree that the fullness of truth was to be found only in Roman Catholicism. But if they did recognize this, they would no longer be where they are. The formula gave Catholics a way of acknowledging the faith of other Christians and even of non-Christians. It motivated them to support these other believers in their faith rather than assail it, as Newman himself had done in some of his early Catholic lectures. By subordinating the acceptance of particular doctrines to the personal dispositions of the believer, Newman was able to perceive the inner dynamics of faith. As he knew from his own experience, it takes time and favorable circumstances to grasp certain doctrinal implications of one's own belief. But at the same time Newman's principle avoids any reductionism. It puts a burden on sincere believers to ponder the apostolic deposit and draw out its meaning and consequences. Inasmuch as the totality of dogma is a single indivisible system, no true doctrine can be dismissed as inconsequential.

Ecumenical strategy

Since ecumenism hardly existed before the twentieth century, it would be anachronistic to speak of Newman as an ecumenist. An outspoken apologist and controversialist on behalf of Catholicism, he was not blind to the values present in other communions. Not infrequently he expressed satisfaction in the common heritage shared by all believers and sought to confirm Christians of every communion in those doctrines and practices that belonged to the general patrimony. In the attitude of faith itself, Newman found an implicit commitment to the entire content of revelation and a promise of healthy growth.

In all his interconfessional dealings Newman held firmly to the principle that everyone is subjectively obliged to follow the biddings of conscience. 'I have always contended,' he once wrote, 'that obedience even to an erring conscience was the way to gain light.'[58] Sensitive to the biddings of conscience, he was on guard against unsettling other Christians in their faith. On the very day of his reception into the Catholic Church he wrote to his sister Jemima that his acceptance of the claims of that Church was entirely 'consistent with believing, as I firmly do, that individuals in the English Church are invisibly knit into that True Body of which they are not outwardly members – and consistent with thinking it highly injudicious, indiscreet, wanton to interfere with them in particular cases ...'[59]

For similar reasons, Newman spoke out against dismissing the historicity of biblical stories that critical historians regarded as inexact or legendary. He lamented the reckless attacks of liberal exegetes on the reliability of the Bible because they deprived conservative Protestants of a needed support. 'To unsettle the minds of a generation, when you give them no landmarks and no causeway across the morass is to undertake a great responsibility.'[60]

Although Newman engaged freely in religious controversy, he observed certain ground rules. Convinced that 'it does not mend matters for us to conceal our mutual differences,' he held that real disagreements ought to be confessed 'plainly though in charity.'[61] He sought always to give a moderate exposition of Catholic doctrine that would not shock or repel the very persons whom one was seeking to persuade. He was particularly opposed to vituperation and personal abuse. Writing on April 13, 1866, to Henry James Coleridge, the Jesuit editor of the *Month*, on the occasion of that journal's response to Pusey's *Eirenicon*, Newman stated: 'Abuse is as great a mistake in controversy as panegyric in biography.'[62] Those who respond to Dr. Pusey, he cautioned, should bear in mind that their aim is to convince readers who respect and love that author.

For many years Newman was in correspondence with Ambrose Phillipps de Lisle, a Catholic layman who espoused a scheme of corporate reunion with the Church of England. Newman judged the scheme unrealistic on the ground that, as we have seen, the ecclesiastical organization of that church was in his view fundamentally Erastian. To make that church genuinely Catholic, Newman believed, would be to fashion a new creature. 'It would be to turn a panther into a hind.'[63]

In 1876 de Lisle favored a scheme to form an Anglican Uniate Church patterned on the Eastern Catholic Churches. Newman expressed sympathy with this effort to draw good people into the Church, but he felt that this complicated plan would not commend itself to the Holy See unless there were a likelihood of bringing in a large portion of the Church of England.[64] The scheme soon collapsed partly because very few Anglo-Catholics were willing to accept the recently defined dogma of papal infallibility and the requirement of conditional reordination of Anglican clergy who would come into union with Rome.[65]

As we have seen, Newman was eager for individual conversions, but he refused to engage in a hunt for converts, and was sometimes accused of a lack of zeal. In his Journal for January 21, 1863, he wrote:

At Propaganda, conversions, and nothing else, are the proof of doing *any* thing. Every where with Catholics, to make converts, is doing something; and not to make them, is 'doing nothing' . . . . But I am altogether different. . . . To me conversions were not the first thing, but the edification of Catholics. . . . I am afraid to make hasty converts of educated men, lest they should not have counted the cost, & should have difficulties after they have entered the Church. . . . [T]he Church must be prepared for converts, as well as converts prepared for the Church.[66]

The governing body of the Church, Newman surmised, was annoyed at his opinion that the Catholics of England were in need of a better education.[67]

While Newman was eager to receive individual converts who were properly prepared, he recognized that some might not have a personal call to take this step. When his friend Samuel F. Wood died in 1843, Newman wrote to his sister Jemima: 'I think he considered the Church of Rome the true Church, – but thought God had placed him where he was' – that is to say, in the Anglican communion.[68] Some decades later Newman speculated that some Anglo-Catholics might be providentially 'kept where they were, with no more light than they have, being Anglicans in good faith in order gradually to prepare their hearers and readers in greater number than would otherwise be possible for the true and perfect faith.'[69] This statement, quite different in tone from some earlier utterances, may reflect the mellowing of Newman in his later years.

Newman does not seem to have had anything resembling a strategy for restoring the unity of Christendom, much as he desired that objective. He was content to take one step at a time. 'Whatever tends to create a unity of heart between men of separate communions,' he wrote, 'lays the ground for advances towards a restoration of that visible unity, the absence of which among Christians is so great a triumph, and so great an advantage to the enemies of the Cross.'[70] Toward the end of his life he became increasingly disturbed at the spread of atheism and irreligion, and as a result came to take greater satisfaction in the partial unity that already existed among religious minds.

> I rejoice in it as one compensation of the cruel overthrow of faith which we see on all sides of us, that, as the setting of the sun brings out the stars, so great principles are found to shine out, which are hailed by men of various religions as their own in common, when infidelity prevails.[71]

In these final years Newman sensed the rise of what we would today call an ecumenical spirit. 'Never did members of the various Christian communions feel such tenderness for each other.'[72] The first step toward unity, Newman believed, must be 'for religious minds, one and all, to live upon the Gospels.'[73] In another letter, written in January 1873 to the same correspondent, he added that the result of the dawning movement toward unity must be placed in

God's hands. The differences are real, and beyond human power to solve. Nevertheless, Newman observed:

> We may hope that our good God has not put into the hearts of religious men to wish and pray for unity, without intending in His own time to fulfill the prayer. ... [W]e may humbly hope that in our day, and till He discloses to the hearts of men what the true faith is, He will, where hearts are honest, take the will [to unity] for the deed.[74]

Newman, we may conclude, was a forerunner, standing on the threshold of a new ecumenical age. In him the convert spoke louder than the ecumenist. But he did succeed in combining a loyal adherence to the Catholic Church with a deep concern for Christian unity and a measure of appreciation for the workings of grace in other Christian communions. His frank and realistic appraisal of the obstacles to union could be a salutary corrective for a generation that is tempted, as ours is, to minimize the distinctive claims of each religious body.

Notes

1   In this chapter I shall draw on materials already published in my article, 'Newman, Conversion, and Ecumenism,' *Theological Studies* 51 (1990), pp. 717–31.

2   Newman, *Certain Difficulties Felt by Anglicans in Catholic Teaching Considered*, 2 vols. (London: Longmans, Green & Co., 1908, 1910), vol. 1, pp. 4, 5, hereafter abbreviated *Diff.*

3   JHN to Miss Rowe, 16 September 1873, in *Letters and Diaries of John Henry Newman*, 31 vols. (London: Nelson, 1961–72 Oxford: Clarendon, 1977–), vol. 26, p. 364, hereafter abbreviated *LD.*

4   JHN to Edward Husband, 17 July 1870, *LD*, vol. 25, p. 161.

5   Newman, *Discourses to Mixed Congregations* (London: Longmans, Green & Co., 1893), p. 20; hereafter abbreviated *Discourses.*

6   *Diff.*, vol. 1, p. 170.

7   Ibid., pp. 170–1.

8   Newman, *Lectures on the Present Position of Catholics in England* (London: Longmans, Green & Co., 1896), p. 35.

9   Ibid., p. 335.

10   Ibid.

11   Ibid.

12   Ibid., pp. 342–3.

13   'Lectures on the History of the Turks' (1853), in *Historical Sketches*, 3 vols. (London: Longmans, Green & Co., 1896), vol. 1, p. 192.

14   Ibid., p. xii; cf. Ian Ker, *John Henry Newman: A Biography* (Oxford: Clarendon, 1989), p. 403.

15   'History of the Turks,' vol. 1, p. 105.

16   *Discourses*, p. 250.

17   *LD*, vol. 18, p. 103–5.

18   *LD*, vol. 25, p. 160.

19   *Diff.*, vol. 1, pp. 86–7.

20   Newman, *Apologia pro Vita Sua* (London: Longmans, Green & Co., 1929), p. 154, referring to four sermons preached at the end of 1843; hereafter abbreviated *Apol.*

21   *LD*, 8, p. 182.

22   Ibid., p. 174.

23   *Diff.*, vol. 1, p. 357.

24   JHN to George T. Edwards, 24 February 1887, *LD*, vol. 31, p. 189.

25   JHN to Helen Douglas Forbes, 4 October 1864, *LD*, vol. 21, p. 249.

26   JHN to Mrs. Lydia Christie, 20 December 1881, *LD*, vol. 30, p. 34.

27   Newman, *Loss and Gain: The Story of a Convert* (London: Longmans, Green & Co., 1896), pp. 381–2.

28   Ibid., p. 382.

29   *Discourses,* p. 177

30   Ibid., p. 178.

31   Ibid., p. 207.

32   Ibid., p. 231.

33   *Diff.*, vol. 1, p. 350.

34   Ibid., pp. 353–4.

35   Ibid., p. 357.

36   Ibid., pp. 358–9.

37   Ibid., p. 188.

38   Ibid., pp. 7–8.

39   Ibid., p. 175.

40   Ibid., p. 65.

41 Ibid., p. 124.

42 JHN to J. M. Capes, 24 December 1850, and 9 February and 18 February 1851, *LD*, 14, p. 173, 207, 213–14.

43 JHN to E. E. Estcourt, 2 June 1860, *LD*, vol. 19, p. 352. This letter was not sent in exactly the same form as here quoted in Newman's draft.

44 *LD*, vol. 20, p. 460.

45 *Apol.*, p. 227, referring to a letter of September 1844.

46 Ibid., pp. 339–42.

47 Ibid., p. 342.

48 Unpublished letter in the archives of the Archdiocese of Philadelphia. Patrick T. Brannan, S.J., presented the full text of this letter in a paper delivered at the Newman Centenary Celebration at the University of Pennsylvania on May 15, 1990.

49 Text in *Diff.*, vol. 2, pp. 1–170, at pp. 9–10. Newman had perhaps forgotten having called the Anglican establishment a 'bulwark' in the letter to Capes of December 24, 1850, mentioned above. But he did guard himself by saying he did not recall what he might have said in a private letter.

50 'The Theory of Developments in Religious Doctrine,' Sermon 15 of Newman's *Fifteen Sermons Preached before the University of Oxford 1826–1843* (third edition, 1871, reprinted London: SPCK, n.d.), p. 336, hereafter abbreviated *OUS*.

51 *Discourses*, p. 261.

52 Newman, *An Essay in Aid of a Grammar of Assent* (London: Longmans, Green & Co., 1901), p. 245.

53 Ibid., pp. 495–501, at p. 499.

54 *Discourses*, p. 261.

55 Ibid., p. 282.

56 Ker, *Newman*, p. 298.

57 *Apol.*, p. 198.

58 JHN to Mrs. William Froude, 4 April 1844; cited in Ker, *Newman*, p. 284.

59 JHN to Mrs. John Mozley, 9 October 1845, *LD*, vol. 11, p. 14.

60 JHN to Malcomb Maccoll, 24 March 1861, *LD*, vol. 20, p. 488.

61 JHN to Principal David Brown, 18 January 1873, *LD*, vol. 26, p. 234.

62 *LD*, vol. 22, p. 211.

63 JHN to Ambrose Phillipps de Lisle 3 March 1866, *LD*, vol. 22, p. 170.

64 JHN to de Lisle, 19 and 27 January 1876, *LD*, vol. 28, pp. 18, 20.

65 Ker, *Newman*, p. 695.

66   Newman, *Autobiographical Writings* (London and New York: Sheed & Ward, 1956), pp. 257–8.

67   Ibid., p. 259.

68   JHN to Mrs. John Mozley, 30 April 1843; quoted in Ker, *Newman*, p. 273.

69   Letter to an unknown correspondent, probably from early 1871; *LD*, vol. 25, p. 260.

70   JHN to Henry Allon, 28 January 1868, *LD*, vol. 24, p. 22.

71   JHN to Principal Brown, 24 January 1875, *LD*, vol. 27, p. 188.

72   JHN to Principal Brown, 24 October 1872, *LD*, vol. 26, p. 187.

73   Ibid., p. 188.

74   JHN to Principal Brown, 3 November 1873, *LD*, vol. 26, p. 381.

9

The University

In 1863 Newman wrote in his private journal: 'Now from first to last, education ... has been my line'[1] Elected a fellow of Oriel College at Oxford in 1822, he served as a tutor for some ten years before embarking on a second career as a churchman and a theologian. After becoming a Catholic in 1845 he maintained that the greatest need of the Catholic Church in England was for education. As an Oratorian he founded and directed a Catholic school for boys in Birmingham. In 1851 the Archbishop of Armagh, Paul Cullen, asked for his help in the founding of a new Catholic University in Ireland, and then offered him the post of Rector. Newman accepted and was formally installed as Rector in June 1854. In 1856 the new university opened, and Newman continued to serve as Rector until 1858, when he resigned, partly because his responsibilities for the Oratory in Birmingham required his full attention and partly because of difficulties arising in Ireland. The Catholic University of Ireland survived until 1882, at which time it was merged into the Royal University of Ireland.

Two years before his installation as Rector, Newman wrote the lectures that constitute the substance of the book now known as *The Idea of a University*. The original collection, published in 1853 with an 1852 imprint was entitled *Discourses on the Scope and Nature of University Education, Addressed to the Catholics of Dublin*, and contained ten lectures. In 1859 Newman published an abbreviated edition, and then in 1873, a larger volume, *The Idea of a University Defined and Illustrated*, which included nine of the original ten discourses and ten additional 'Lectures and Essays,' previously published as a separate volume in 1859. This book, although it seems to have aroused little interest in Newman's lifetime, has since been widely hailed as a classic. Walter Pater spoke of it as 'the perfect handling of a theory.'[2] James M. Cameron, writing in 1977, called it 'the most influential (I suppose) book yet written on university education.'[3] Jaroslav Pelikan, in his *The Idea of the University*, calls it 'the most important book ever written about the university.'[4] Newman's *Idea* particularly calls for attention in the present work because it expresses much of his deepest thinking about theology in its relationship to other disciplines such as philosophy, literature, and the natural sciences. Instead of attempting a summary, I shall here select several major themes.

The crisis of the University

The educational crisis addressed in Newman's *Idea* is one that had broken out while he was a tutor at Oxford. It was occasioned by two major developments: the turn against the classics and the rejection of religion as an academic subject.

The opposition to the classics was spearheaded by the utilitarian school in philosophy, especially Lord Henry Brougham, Sydney Smith, and the editors of the *Edinburgh Review*. These writers, following in the footsteps of John Locke and Jeremy Bentham, wished to dethrone the classics from their position of eminence and replace them with useful knowledge leading to a trade or profession (pp. 158–63).[5] The exclusion of theology was being urged by many of the same theorists and was implemented in the newly founded University of London, which allowed no place for religion in its curriculum. Newman blamed this secularist trend partly on Evangelicalism, which looked upon religion not as knowledge but as a matter of sentiment (pp. 27–8). If religion were simply a praiseworthy feeling, like motherly love or patriotism, one could not reasonably demand a chair for it in the university (p. 29). But for Newman, as we shall see, religion was a matter of truth.

Newman was profoundly worried by what he foresaw as the long-term results of this two-pronged assault on classical wisdom and Christian faith. The center was not holding. In the absence of any integrating principle, the curriculum was being dismembered (pp. 26, 69). Each discipline, pressing for its own point of view, was making excessive claims for itself (pp. 73–96). New courses dealing with modern sciences and professions, were proliferating. In an attempt to keep up with the growth of factual knowledge, he contended, universities were substituting particular skills and information for true education (pp. 113–14). The student, forced to memorize the findings of many disciplines, was condemned to superficiality (p. 142).

'In the race for popularity and power' (p. 403) the new sciences, dealing with tangible facts and recent discoveries, were continually gaining ground. But these specialized disciplines, according to Newman, failed to deal with the human in its full dimensions. Rather, they tended to reduce the human to what could be handled by their own methods – those of physics, chemistry, biology, psychology, medicine, economics, or whatever (pp. 512–13). Academic specialization and professionalization were being re-inforced by the trend in society to reduce the worth of individuals to their function in the process of production and consumption (p. 168).

The truth that unifies

In addressing the crisis of fragmentation Newman avoids a strategy of exclusion. All the modern sciences and learned professions, he maintains, have a legitimate place in the university. In his university at Dublin, he set up not only a school of arts and sciences but also schools of medicine and engineering, making provision for a chemical laboratory and an astronomical observatory.[6] This inclusiveness was necessary because the university, according to the concept Newman accepted, was a seat of universal learning (pp. 19–20, 457).

The problem is not so much the existence of multiple disciplines as the lack of coordination. Each discipline, Newman believed, tended to make itself the center of all truth, neglecting or rejecting what did not fall within its purview. But this one-sidedness was not incorrigible. Because reality is a single, undivided whole (p. 51), and because the object of knowledge is truth as such, all knowledge forms 'one large system or complex fact' (p. 45). To grasp reality in its wholeness and unity we need to have not only objects but intellectual eyes that can perceive relationships (p. 144). This ability is not inborn; it is acquired through training and discipline of mind.

The main point of education, as Newman understands it, is to impart this capacity to get a connected grasp of the real in its full range. He draws an analogy between the university and the student.

The university, because it deals with the whole body of knowledge, is like an empire made up of many nationalities. It 'maps out the territory of the intellect, and sees that the boundaries of each province are religiously respected, and that there is neither encroachment nor surrender on any side. ... It is impartial toward them all, and promotes each in its own place and for its own object' (p. 459). Where such order prevails, education can impart 'the clear, calm, accurate vision and comprehension of all things, as far the finite mind can embrace them, each in its own place' (p. 139).

This quality of mind is what Newman calls the 'imperial intellect' (p. 461) or the 'philosophical habit of mind' (p. 51). It is, he contends, 'the special fruit of the education furnished at a University' (p. 102). Philosophy, as he uses the term, is not simply another discipline, parallel to the special arts and sciences; it is rather what some today might call a 'second-order' discipline, or, in Newman's own terminology, 'Thought or Reason exercised upon Knowledge' (p. 139). Philosophy is, so to speak, the form of knowledge (p. 179). In the original Discourse V (present in the 1852 edition but omitted from later editions), Newman holds that philosophy, rather than theology or any other discipline, 'embraces and locates truth of every kind, and every method of attaining it.'[7] It corresponds in many respects to what we commonly understand as wisdom, which does not coincide with either philosophy or theology as a special discipline, but imparts an overarching view of reality as known from reason and revelation in unison.

Newman's description of philosophy as the 'form' of knowledge seemed to be at variance with a brief issued by Pope Pius IX in 1854, which exhorts the bishops to make 'our divine religion as it were the soul of all instruction in letters' ('*divina nostra religio tamquam anima totius litterariae institutionis*'). In an autobiographical memorandum of his connection with the Catholic University, Newman later remarked: 'I wrote on a different idea in my 'Discourses on University Education' in 1852, vid especially the original 5th Discourse.'[8] The difference of terminology between Newman and the Pope does not seem to amount to a real disagreement, since Newman himself, in a footnote to the 1852 edition, wrote: 'It would be possible to call Theology the *external* form of the philosophical system, as charity has been said to be of living faith,' but he adds that in that case theology would not be one of the sciences, but a form of them all.[9] Some authors speculate that the appearance of a disagreement with the Pope may have been one motive for Newman's omission of the original Discourse V in later editions.

Newman's point about the formative role of philosophy is of course unacceptable to utilitarians. They assert that such cultivation of mind, although it may prepare students for a life of leisure, does not equip them for any trade or profession, and is consequently useless. Newman's answer is twofold. In the first place he argues that knowledge, as a perfection of the intellect, is its own end. He quotes Cicero to the effect that truth is something all people desire for its own sake (p. 104). In the second place, Newman argues, liberal education is useful insofar as it equips the student to enter into many trades and professions. A person with a sharpened mental vision can become a better orator, statesman, soldier, lawyer, or physician than one who lacks such education (pp. 165–6).

A further point in Newman's argument is that the study of the classics – that is to say, the poets, historians, and philosophers of Greece and Rome – has proved its capacity 'to strengthen, refine, and enrich the intellectual powers,' whereas the study of the experimental sciences has not been shown to accomplish this purpose (p. 263). He also argues that the ancient classics, along with biblical revelation, lie at the foundation of the common civilization of the cultivated world (pp. 250–4). In the course of time Rome became the heir to the wisdom of Athens and to the grace that radiated from Jerusalem. The two have been fused into a complex whole, which Newman took to be a civilization without rival on the face of the earth. In his own words, 'To separate those distinct teachings, human and divine, which meet in Rome, is to retrograde; it is to rebuild the Jewish Temple and to plant anew the groves of Academus' (p. 265).

The light of faith

Thus far we have seen no grounds for asserting that a university should concern itself with revelation, faith, theology, or Catholicism. Yet these concerns are central to Newman's thought. He argues primarily from the nature of the university as a seat of universal learning and from the interconnectedness of all truth. If the university purports to teach universal knowledge, he reasons, it cannot exclude theology, unless it be denied that theology is a significant field of knowledge (p. 21). For Catholics, at least, it is evident that something can be known about God, that such knowledge is important, and that theological truths can be built into a system (p. 61). The reality of God is borne in upon us by testimony, by history, by induction, by metaphysics, and by the experience of conscience (pp. 25–6). Admittedly divine truth is different in kind from merely human truth, but so do human truths differ in kind from one another (p. 26). Such qualitative difference does not give grounds for exclusion.

To relegate the study of God to a professional school of divinity would be unwarranted because theology has implications for other sciences. 'If there be Religious Truth at all,' writes Newman, 'we cannot shut our eyes to it without prejudice to truth of every kind, physical, metaphysical, historical, and moral; for it bears upon all truth' (p. 52). So important is theology that its absence creates a void that other disciplines then seek to fill, even though they lack the necessary competence. They will often fill the gap with conclusions that do not harmonize with Christian faith. For example, historians who overlook God's mighty deeds in biblical history will often reason as though the whole course of worldly events were determined by inner-worldly causes (p. 85). Economists will theorize as though the chief end of human activity were the increase of wealth, whereas revelation warns against the dangers of loving money and inculcates the value of voluntary poverty (pp. 86–7). Medicine will be taught as though health and longevity were the highest goods, although the gospel instructs us that we should not fear those who kill the body and that we should be ready to lay down our lives for a holy cause (p. 88).

Some might propose that only natural theology ought to be taught in the university, leaving revealed theology to the parish or seminary.[10] Up to a point Newman agrees, because the philosophy of education can be founded to a great extent on truths of the natural order that may be held by theists of all denominations (pp. 4–7). Seeking to reach out to a broader audience, Newman in his first few lectures dwells by preference on theological truths that can be established by unaided reason (p. 69). But he hastens to add that no Catholic can tolerate the omission of revealed facts and principles that go far beyond natural reason and are known by faith to be most true (ibid.). In later chapters he makes the point that in the fallen condition of humanity, reason will quickly go astray unless it submits to the guidance of faith (pp. 181–2).

Within the sphere of faith Newman refuses to limit university instruction to apologetics or to doctrines that the majority of Christians hold in common as distinct from doctrines specific to Catholicism. His basic principle is that 'Catholicism is one whole, and admits of no compromise or modification' (p. 182). There is no such thing, he says, as religion in general or Christianity in general.[11] In the Catholic framework each doctrine is affected by its relationship to all the others. Our doctrine of God is influenced by the Incarnation, and our doctrine of the Incarnation is influenced by our understanding of Mary, the Church, and the Eucharist. No part of Catholic truth, therefore, can be set aside.

Newman thus arrives at a conclusion that must have seemed almost as astonishing to his audience as it does to us today: 'A University, so called, which refuses to profess the Catholic Creed, is, from the nature of the case, hostile both to the Church and to Philosophy.'[12] In another lecture he puts the same thought in other words: 'If the Catholic faith is true, a University cannot exist externally to the Catholic pale' (p. 214).

These provocative statements need to be rightly understood. Newman is not denying the weakness of many Catholic universities. He would, I suppose, admit that an Anglican, Protestant, or nondenominational university, or for that matter a Muslim university, could outrank a given Catholic university in imparting the disciplines of science, literature, law, and economics, or in imbuing its students with a philosophical cast of mind. He is speaking of the idea of the university, and in this context he wishes to emphasize the beneficent influence of revealed truth, in its Catholic form, upon the university as such. Where no account is taken of divine revelation and its interpretation in the Catholic tradition, the university will be deficient precisely as a university. With this bold assertion he puts the secularists and liberals on the defensive.

Newman makes distinctions between the kinds of theology to be imparted respectively to professional students of divinity and to lay students. The university, he reminds his hearers, is not a seminary; it is a place to fit men of the world for the world (p. 232). For secular students he insists on what he calls 'general religious knowledge,' similar to that customarily taught in the school of arts at most English universities. It would be a reproach, even a scandal, for a Catholic university to send its graduates into the world accomplished in all knowledge except Christian knowledge.

It might be objected at this point that faith is a personal response to divine grace, and that it cannot be imparted by academic instruction. As we have seen from his letters opposing the reading room at Tamworth, Newman was quite aware of this difficulty.[13] In his *Idea of a University* he deftly avoids the problem by maintaining that in the school of philosophy and letters religion should be taught simply as a branch of knowledge. Because religious knowledge was an important aspect of the course of study, it should be a matter for examinations. The student should be expected to have no less familiarity with biblical literature than with classical literature, and to be no less cognizant of sacred history than of profane history (pp. 372–6). Although correct information cannot of itself produce Catholic faith, it can dissolve many of the intellectual obstacles to it.

With regard to doctrine, Newman contents himself with conveying a broad knowledge of matters treated in the catechism and the religious topics with which lay persons actually have to deal, including the controverted issues that commonly arise in discussions with Protestants. Newman speaks in this connection of Christian knowledge in its secular aspect, that which is practically useful in the course of life and in general conversation, including studies that bear on the history, the literature, and the philosophy of Christianity. But he would exclude the teaching *in extenso* of pure dogma. He warns that a lawyer, physician, statesman, or merchant who sets about discussing theological points is no more likely to succeed than an ecclesiastic who meddles with law, medicine, or finance.

The role of ecclesiastical authority

For Newman the university is not a mere instrument of the Church. It requires a measure of autonomy because it has its own proper end, distinct from that of the Church. Its specific aim is not the salvation of souls but higher education. Returning to a metaphor mentioned above, Newman speaks of the university as having imperial authority. It exercises sovereignty over the various disciplines, maps out their respective territories, and adjudicates disputes among them. But the sovereignty of the university, in Newman's view, is limited. Insofar as grace and revelation are superior to nature and reason, the Church, which is sovereign in speaking about these higher realms, has a certain authority over the Catholic university. The infallible pronouncements of the Church must be accepted without question (p. 459).

When the Church founds a university, Newman declares, she does so not for the sake of pure knowledge but for the spiritual welfare and religious influence of her members (p. xii). Beyond the specific finality of the university lies a spiritual aim not specific to the university as such.

141

This double finality, proximate and final, creates a situation of tension of which Newman is acutely conscious. Just as the secular state, pursuing its own proper end, sometimes comes into conflict with the Church, so likewise does the university. The cultivation of knowledge, he says, exerts a subtle influence upon our habits of thought, making us treat our own minds as the measure of all things (p. 217). Absolutizing its own standards and goals, the university tends to become a rival of the Church even in the territory entrusted to the Church itself. To prevent this encroachment, the Church must exercise what Newman calls 'a direct and active jurisdiction' over the university (p. 215). This jurisdiction is especially needed because the phenomena on which morality and religion are based do not present themselves with luminous evidence. Since we have only faint intimations of the spiritual world, we need a government here on earth to guide our perceptions of it. The university, because it concerns itself with the whole realm of knowledge, stands in need of direction from a universal religious authority. 'That great institution, then, the Catholic Church, has been set up by Divine Mercy, as a present visible antagonist, and the only possible antagonist, to sight and sense.' The world, a stubborn opponent of spiritual truth, has no adequate opponent except the Catholic Church, which is the sole undaunted champion to vindicate the moral order and keep us loyal to it (pp. 515–16).

Newman illustrates the danger of infidelity in the realm of theology, where the Church has special responsibility. Theology in the university, he observes, is easily drawn into rationalism or skepticism. The urge to construct a complete system of truth 'gives birth to a rebellious stirring against miracle and mystery, against the severe and the terrible' (p. 218). Even the medieval universities, operating under ecclesiastical vigilance, were infected with various forms of rationalism, as the condemnations of Abelard, Roscellinus, and David of Dinant bear witness (p. 384).[14] Since the university cannot fulfill its mission without benefit of revealed truth, the Church must be present to see that this truth is sincerely and integrally acknowledged (p. 227). It must correct distortions or dilutions of the gospel.

The loyal Catholic, according to Newman, accepts the dogmas of the faith without hesitation. They impede true thought as little as the laws of physics impede our bodily movements (p. 471). Often, however, new theological opinions arise which run counter to the opinions of weighty authorities. Provided that revealed truth is not contested, some elbow-room must be granted for speculation. Every intellectual triumph in the history of theology, as we have noted in Chapter 7, has been preceded by a period of controversy (pp. 475–6). Patience is needed in allowing academic thinkers to reach conclusions by their own methods. When the inquiry is conducted with a loyal Catholic spirit and a deep sense of responsibility, we may be sure that theological speculation will not be injurious to faith. 'Error may flourish for a while, but Truth will prevail in the end' (p. 478).

Although the Church has a responsibility to watch over theology, she has no direct concern with secular science (p. 227). Scientists must, however, be challenged when they exceed their proper domain and trespass on the territory of faith. In several chapters on Christianity and scientific investigation, Newman shows his awareness of the extreme delicacy of questions in which faith and science may seem to collide. He is confident that the difficulties can be ironed out in time, provided that there is patience and good will on both sides. Truth, he asserts, cannot be contrary to truth (p. 446).

Somewhat different in character is the Church's office toward literature. The university is not a seminary or a convent. In teaching secular literature, Newman maintains, the university does not intend so much to edify students as to prepare them for life in the real world (p. 232). As the voice of fallen humanity, literature exhibits men and women as they are, both at their best and at their worst. Without wishing the Church to protrude herself as censor, Newman grants that she must sometimes exercise her authority to prevent the faithful from being misled or confused by injudicious reading (p. 234).

The reader may be surprised that Newman in his lectures devotes very little attention to the moral formation and pastoral care of students. He insists that the business of the university is knowledge, not morality or piety. But he does expect teachers to exercise a formative influence and inspire their students to a better life. The university, as he conceives it, has colleges, that is to say, places of residence in which students are placed under the guidance and instruction of superiors and tutors, who are concerned with their moral and spiritual development as persons. In another work, 'The Rise and Progress of Universities,' Newman emphasized the importance of the personal influence of the tutor to supplement the academic instruction of the professor.[15]

Evaluation

The Idea of a University, like much of Newman's other work, is very subtly argued. The author treads on a very fine line between mutually opposed positions. He strikes a balance between the autonomy of reason and the sovereignty of faith and between the value of contemplation and the need to train students for practical life in the world. It is hard to tell whether he is more opposed to a liberalism that allows unaided reason to chart its own course or a clerical authoritarianism that suffocates free intellectual inquiry. Different chapters give different emphases, but Newman does not contradict himself. At no point does he lose sight of the polarities.

Some critics have accused Newman of inconsistencies. A. Dwight Culler, in his valuable study of the subject,[16] holds that Newman, because of his ambivalence toward intellectual culture, retracts in Discourse IX the glowing praise for intellectual refinement expressed in the two preceding Discourses. With some exaggeration, says Culler, one might find two authors composing the humanistic and religious discourses in the *Idea* – the first being the liberal disciple of Richard Whately the Oxford logician, and the second, the doctrinaire protégé of Walter Mayers, committed only to the word of God. But Newman had long since worked through this tension without eliminating it, as we have seen in our study of the Oxford University Sermons. Rejecting the Evangelical notion that faith and reason were mutually opposed, he adopted the view that reason was open to faith and fulfilled in faith. But, conscious of the proneness of human reason to fall captive to pride and self-interest, Newman saw the need for submission to the authority of divine revelation. These themes, pervasive in Newman's writings, show up again in *The Idea of a University*. He recognizes both the value of reason in interpreting the data of experience and the danger of rationalism. For this reason he insists on a real though limited autonomy for the university and on its subordination to the higher jurisdiction of the Church. Without ecclesiastical affiliation the Catholic university would lack an important source of its distinctive strength.

Newman's *Idea*, published a century and a half ago, needs to be taken up in a new context today. Perhaps no better point of comparison can be found than the teaching of John Paul II, who has spoken frequently on the subject of Catholic higher education. In his apostolic constitution *Ex corde Ecclesiae* (1990), he quotes several times from *The Idea of a University*.[17]

John Paul II describes the crisis of the university in terms reminiscent of Newman. It is, he says, a crisis of truth and alienation. In modern technological society, he points out, the individual tends to be reduced to the status of an instrument. Educational institutions are under pressure to turn out an efficient work force for production[18] or a body of skilled professionals rather than to satisfy the quest for truth and goodness.[19] In a mechanized and consumerist society the ethical is subordinated to the technical, the spiritual to the material, and the order of being to that of having.[20]

In this situation, says the Pope, the university tends to become fragmented into independent sectors.[21] The curriculum is in danger of being reduced to a collection of specialized disciplines that are 'in the end, inarticulate and unrelated.'[22] A rich human formation is too often lacking. The multiplication of departments, faculties and institutes, will not suffice to overcome the crisis of the university.

Modern science aggravates the problem by tending to reduce the human to what can be measured and to frustrate the innate quest of the human mind for a truth that can bring unity and purpose into human lives.[23] The university should fan this desire into flame. It should challenge its students not to be satisfied with a passive reception of the doctrine handed out to them but to continue their search for truth and meaning throughout their lives.[24]

John Paul II, like Newman, proposes to solve the problem of fragmentation by communicating an organic vision of reality in which everything has its due place.[25] 'The university is meant to be a 'living unity' of individual organisms dedicated to the research into truth.'[26] It must offer a higher synthesis in which the whole range of universal truth is taken into account.[27] A 'universal humanism,' he asserts, can assure respect for the human person as the only created being that exists for its own sake.[28] Mindful of the limitations of science, the university can help to order scientific progress for the benefit of humanity.[29] The heart and soul of the university is 'truth as something researched, loved, taught, and promulgated.'[30] Truth, in the last analysis, is not an impersonal abstraction but a person who comes to us in the flesh of Jesus Christ. Christ the Logos, as the center of creation and of human history, must enlighten the university.[31]

The Catholic university, says John Paul II, is uniquely fitted to promote that 'united endeavor of intelligence and faith' which will 'enable people to come to the full measure of their humanity' and understand themselves as created to the image of God and as called in Christ to eternal life.[32] This Christian orientation enables the university to include moral and spiritual considerations in its research and evaluation of science and technology.[33]

Like Newman, John Paul II holds that theology plays a central role in the synthesis of knowledge and in the dialogue between faith and reason. The study of philosophy and theology should enable students to acquire an organic vision of reality and prepare them to give the witness of their faith in the world.[34]

Like Newman, again, John Paul II maintains that Catholic universities must have an institutional bond with the Church, to which the revelation of Christ has been entrusted.[35] He expects the 'Catholic' character of the universities to be visible and open, so that it can inform their structures and programs.[36]

Apart from these important convergences, three main differences may be noted between our two authors. Unlike Newman, John Paul II does not identify civilization with the culture that stems from Greece and Rome. As a Pole, he recognizes that even in Europe the culture of the Slavic world provides a true alternative. In his worldwide travels he emphasizes that the gospel cannot be identified with any single culture and that every culture has a part to play in the universal plan of salvation.[37] Although the Church cannot forsake what she has gained from her inculturation in the world of Greco-Roman thought, she may be further enriched by dialogue with other cultures.[38]

A second difference has to do with the relative prominence of teaching and research. Newman in his *Idea* presents the university almost exclusively as a teaching institution. John Paul II, however, expects the university to serve the Church and secular society by its scholarly research and by its evaluation of the achievements of science and technology.[39] Partly because of his neglect of the functions of research and publication, Newman's book has had less influence on universities than on relatively small religiously-oriented colleges.

The third difference has to do with the responsibility of the university for the moral and pastoral care of students. Whereas Newman in his *Idea of a University* emphasized almost exclusively the intellectual aspect of education, John Paul II attributes a pastoral as well as an academic function to the university. Through its pastoral ministry programs, he says, the university should take care of the spiritual needs of the students and form them to participate actively in the life of the Church and in service to the larger society.[40] Newman, of course, was not insensitive to this concern. The idea of the spiritual responsibility of the tutor was, in fact, the heart of his disagreement with Edward Hawkins at Oriel. When he wrote the *Idea*, he continued to look upon the moral and pastoral training of students as a responsibility of colleges and tutors rather than the university as such.

While issues such as these three may continue to be debated, the lasting importance of Newman's masterly work remains unimpaired. In insisting on the cognitive value of faith and on the importance of philosophy and theology for the integration of knowledge, Newman presents a challenge to Catholic universities in the English-speaking world and everywhere.

Notes

1   Newman, *Autobiographical Writings* (New York: Sheed & Ward, 1957), p. 259.

2   Walter Pater, *Appreciations with an Essay on Style* (London: Macmillan, 1890), p. 18.

3   J. M. Cameron, *On the Idea of a University* (Toronto: University of Toronto Press, 1978), p. xi.

4   Jardslav Pelikan, *The Idea of the University: A Reexamination* (New Haven: Yale University Press, 1992), p. 190.

5   Newman, *The Idea of A University Defined and Illustrated*, ed. Ian T. Ker (Oxford: Clarendon, 1976). In my text the numbers in parentheses referring to this work refer to page numbers in the uniform edition (London: Longmans, Green & Co., 1889). Ker indicates these page numbers in the margins of his edition. Henceforth abbreviated *Idea*.

6   For details see Fergal McGrath, *The Consecration of Learning: Lectures on Newman's Idea of a University* (New York: Fordham University Press, 1962), pp. 211–26.

7   *Idea*, Ker edn, p. 428.

8   *Autobiographical Writings*, p. 323.

9   *Idea*, Ker edn, p. 428, footnote.

10   This impression might be given by Jaroslav Pelikan's article 'Ex corde Universitatis: Reflections on the Significance of Newman's "Insisting Solely on Natural Theology"' in *Catholic Universities in Church and Society*, ed. John P. Langan (Washington, DC: Georgetown University Press, 1993), pp. 196–209.

11   *Idea*, Original Discourse V, Ker edn, pp. 419–34, at p. 429.

12   Ibid., p. 434.

13 See above, Chapter 3, at footnote 10.

14 See in this connection Newman's essay, 'The Strength and Weakness of Universities: Abelard,' Chapter 16 of 'Rise and Progress of Universities,' *Historical Sketches*, 3 vols. (London: Longmans, Green & Co., 1896), vol. 3, pp. 192–202.

15 See especially the essay 'Professors and Tutors,' Chapter 15 of 'The Rise and Progress,' ibid., vol. 3, pp. 179–92. Here he makes the point that colleges pertain not to the essence but to the integrity of the university. Along the same lines, Newman wrote in a letter of July 23, 1852 to David Moriarty: '*I do not think that a University has to do with morals* as it *has* to do with faith (under the name of knowledge) – nor do I think that the Church on the whole employs a University for morals (except as *teaching* them, but *that* comes under faith –) but I think she uses small bodies in the Universities, Colleges, Halls, etc. etc. as the preservative of *morals*, more naturally.' *The Letters and Diaries of John Henry Newman*, 31 Vols. (London: Nelson, 1961–72, Oxford: Clarendon 1977–); hereafter abbreviated *LD*. vol. 15, p. 136.

16 A. Dwight Culler, *The Imperial Intellect: A Study of Newman's Educational Ideal* (New Haven: Yale University Press, 1955), pp. 226–9, 258–9, *et passim*.

17 John Paul II, 'The Apostolic Constitution on Catholic Universities,' *Origins* 20 (October 4, 1990), pp. 265–76. See pp. 275–6, notes 7 and 19. This apostolic constitution will hereafter be referred to as *Ex corde*, followed by paragraph number or, if reference is being made to the General Norms, to the numbered article.

18 John Paul II, 'On the Catholic Universities,' Address to the Third International Meeting of Catholic Universities and Institutions of Higher Learning, Vatican City, April 25, 1989; text in *Acta Apostolicae Sedis* [AAS] 81 (1989), pp. 1216–25, §3, at p. 1218; English translations in *The Pope Speaks* 34 (1989), pp. 261–72; §3, at p. 218. References to this speech will be given as 'Vatican,' followed by the section number from the AA edition.

19 John Paul II, 'Excellence, Truth, and Freedom in Catholic Universities,' Address at The Catholic University, Washington, DC, October 6, 1979, *Origins* 9 (October 25, 1979), pp. 306–8, §5, p. 307.

20 *Ex corde*, p. 18.

21 Vatican, §4.

22 Ibid.

23 John Paul II, Address at Institut Catholique, Paris, June 1, 1980, *Origins* 10 (June 12, 1980), pp. 52–8, margins, at p. 53.

24 *Ex corde*, para. 23.

25 *Ex corde*, para. 20.

26 Vatican, §4.

27 *Ex corde*, paras. 4 and 16.

28 *Ex corde*, para. 4.

29   Vatican, §6a.

30   Vatican, §4.

31   *Ex corde*, para. 16.

32   *Ex corde*, para. 5.

33   *Ex corde*, para. 7.

34   *Ex corde*, paras. 19–20.

35   *Ex corde*, para. 13; General Norms, art. 2.

36   *Ex corde*, paras. 13–14; General Norms, art. 2; Vatican, §9.

37   John Paul II, Address at the University of Coimbra, Portugal, May 15, 1982, §5; text in *L'Osservatore Romano* (English language edn), 5 July 1982, p. 6; also Encyclical *Slavorum apostoli*, §27; text in *Origins* 15 (July 18, 1985), pp. 113–35, at p. 123.

38   John Paul II, Encyclical *Fides et Ratio*, p. 72.

39   *Ex corde*, para. 7.

40   *Ex corde*, paras. 38–42.

10

Newman in retrospect

Newman at times denied that he was a theologian. In 1867 he wrote to a Jesuit theologian: 'It is not often that I have attempted to discuss any point of pure theology, controversy being rather my line of writing.'[1] Partly on that ground he excused himself from accepting an invitation to attend the First Vatican Council. At the time he wrote to a friend: 'Really and truly I am not a theologian.'[2] Possibly he meant that his primary interest was not in systematic theology. Even his *Lectures on Justification* are in great part polemical. His most enduring contributions were in the realm of what we today call fundamental theology. He was not only an apologist and controversialist, but also a highly original explorer of theological method. Three of his books are notable in this regard. In his *University Sermons* he gradually worked out a balanced position on the problem of faith and reason. In his *Essay on Development* he established the fact that dogma evolves in history; in addition, he provided a set of helpful tests for distinguishing between authentic developments and doctrinal corruptions. In his *Grammar of Assent* he called attention to the vital importance of informal reasoning and the operations of what he called the 'illative sense.' Contributions such as these have earned Newman a distinguished niche in the gallery of great theologians.

Comparison with Vatican II

In our own day students of Newman will want to know how his

achievement stands up in the light of subsequent reflection and changed conditions. The Second Vatican Council, which dealt a century later with many of the same questions with which Newman wrestled, offers a convenient point of comparison. Vatican II is sometimes hailed as 'the Council of John Henry Newman.'[3] No less an authority than Pope Paul VI said that Vatican II could be called in a special way 'Newman's hour.'[4] Ian Ker, a leading expert, remarks that Newman has often been called the "Father" of the Second Vatican Council, but he admits: 'It might be difficult or impossible to trace his direct influence on the actual council documents.'[5] Nicholas Lash, still more cautiously, holds that 'Newman had little direct influence on what took place at Vatican II,' and dismisses 'the myth of 'Newman's council.'"[6]

For any fruitful comparison it would be necessary to consider what Newman and Vatican II intended respectively to achieve. Newman's life was dedicated in great part to the defense of dogmatic religion and of a living, infallible teaching office. He loved the Church of the Fathers, that of Athanasius and of the Council of Nicaea. In his *biglietto* speech, delivered on the occasion of his elevation to the cardinalate, he described opposition to the spirit of liberalism as the main theme of his life's work.

These statements, like most generalizations about Newman, call for immediate qualification. Even in his most ardent apologias for Roman primacy one can detect a subtle undercurrent of criticism. Wary of despotism and ultramontane power politics, he was strongly committed to the inviolability of conscience, the dignity of the laity, and the freedom of theological investigation.

Vatican II is widely perceived as a council of liberalization. It has been generally interpreted as having relaxed the tensions between Catholicism and the contemporary world. While stoutly reaffirming the teaching of Vatican I on papal primacy, it gave greater scope to the free initiatives of bishops, local churches, and lay persons. In its statements on sociopolitical issues, the Council is frequently read (or misread) as endorsing democratic trends and supporting liberty, equality, and fraternity, the slogans of the French Revolution.

In the most general terms, Vatican II can be described as having had two principal goals, summed up respectively in the French word *ressourcement* and the Italian word *aggiornamento*. On the one hand, it promoted a return to the sources, Scripture and the Fathers. On the other hand, it sought to update the Church and bring it into the modern world.

Newman, I submit, would have applauded the return to

Christian antiquity, but he would have been cautious about the 'updating' of the Church. He felt a passionate love for Scripture and the Fathers. The trinitarian and christological dogmas of the early councils were foundational to his faith. But with equal passion he excoriated the principles of the French Revolution and of scientific positivism. The modern world, in his view, was rapidly heading toward simple unbelief. The Church, he believed, ought to combat the spirit of modernity, making use of its infallible teaching authority as needed to throw back what he called 'the immense energy of the aggressive, capricious, untrustworthy intellect.'[7]

Turning more to particulars, we may compare Newman's thinking with the teaching of Vatican II on a series of common themes, ranging from revelation and faith through ecclesiology to sociopolitical questions.

Revelation and faith

With regard to revelation, Newman and Vatican II are remarkably concordant. They both pick up from the Fathers the idea that God speaks to humanity through his Word, the eternal Logos, who became incarnate in Jesus Christ. Revelation according to Newman is not simply a collection of propositional truths but, more fundamentally, the impression made on the human mind by the self-communication of God as Logos. He would probably agree with Vatican II that Jesus Christ himself is the mediator and the fullness of all revelation.[8] The Incarnation, he holds, is the central idea of Christianity. The life of Christ, he says, collects the scattered rays of light that were poured over the face of creation from the beginning.[9]

Both Newman and Vatican II picked up from the early Fathers the idea that 'seeds of the Word' were disseminated far and wide throughout the religions of the world and that fragments of revelation were transmitted through the traditions of what Newman called paganism. Vatican II, while avoiding the term 'paganism,' made much of the 'seeds of the Word' and suggested, as did Newman, that they might have salvific value for peoples who had not been evangelized.[10]

Although it would be possible to construct several different definitions of faith on the basis of Newman's writings, his most fundamental insight would seem to be that faith results from a kind of interior inclination or supernatural instinct whereby we recognize and adhere to the self-manifestation of God in history. He also insisted that faith is not a notional but a real assent – a commitment involving the whole person. This view of faith coheres closely with the teaching of Vatican II, which described faith as the obedience whereby one entrusts one's whole self to God under the sway of the Holy Spirit working in the human heart.

Within this similarity, however, a contrast must be noted. Newman was quintessentially an apologist. He spent much of his career seeking to establish the harmony between faith and reason. This problem, inherited from the Enlightenment, was treated in some detail by Vatican I during Newman's own lifetime, but was studiously ignored by Vatican II. Whereas Newman wrote at length about miracles, Vatican II virtually ignored these and other signs of credibility. Refraining from anything resembling apologetics, Vatican II gave little attention to the role of reason in preparing the way to faith.

Pope John Paul II, however, expresses the relationship between faith and reason in terms reminiscent of Newman. In a message to the Archbishop of Birmingham on the second centenary of Newman's birth, the Pope praised Newman's 'remarkable synthesis of faith and reason,' comparing it to what he himself had previously described as the 'two wings on which the human spirit rises to the contemplation of the truth.'[11] Like Newman, the Pope emphasizes personal trust in living witnesses and the attraction of transcendent truth, which alone can assuage the craving of the human heart. For John Paul, as for Newman, the Blessed Virgin Mary provides a model for theologians contemplating the truths of revelation.

Scripture and tradition

Newman retained from his Protestant and Anglican roots a deep love of Holy Scripture, which he regarded as an infallible and inspired record of revealed truth. He wrestled long and hard with the problem of reconciling the inspiration of Scripture with its apparent errors in the realms of science and history. His efforts to exempt incidental details (which he called *obiter dicta*) from the full effects of inspiration, as noted in Chapter 5, may not have been fully satisfactory, but they can be interpreted as anticipating Vatican II, which taught that Scripture is inerrant in teaching 'that truth which God wanted put into the sacred writings for the sake of our salvation.'[12]

On the interpretation of Scripture, Newman was enamored of the Alexandrian Fathers and suspicious of modern historical criticism, which he regarded as a fruit of German rationalism. He was convinced that 'the mystical interpretation and orthodoxy stand or fall together.'[13] In this he can hardly claim the support of Vatican II, which encouraged scholars to pursue the literal sense by studying the text in its own historical and cultural context. The Council did not speak of mystical or spiritual senses, but it did call for attention to the unity of Scripture as a whole and to the living tradition of the Church as guides to the full meaning of the sacred text.[14] These assertions would have gratified Newman.

Both Newman and Vatican II treated the question of the sufficiency of Scripture. As a Protestant Newman had held that all revealed truth is somehow contained in Scripture,[15] but that Scripture could not be adequately understood except in the light of tradition.[16] Writing as a Catholic, he was inclined to believe that there were revealed truths knowable only by tradition, but he continued to hold that the whole of revelation could be found in Scripture in some sense, either literal or mystical.[17] He added that the living authority of the magisterium must also be reckoned with in settling debated points of exegesis.[18] Here Newman and Vatican II speak in harmony. Both agree on the inseparability of Scripture, tradition, and magisterium and on the fact that the Church does not derive its full assurance about all revealed truth from the Bible alone.[19]

Development of doctrine

The principle of the development of doctrine, pioneered by Newman, came to be universally accepted in the Catholic Church by the end of the nineteenth century. Vatican II invokes this principle in its Declaration on Religious Freedom and expounds it, albeit briefly, in the Constitution on Revelation. It should be noted, however, that Newman's use of the principle was defensive and apologetic. He wanted to show that the Catholic Church of his time was in continuity with that of the Apostles and the Fathers. Vatican II, on the contrary, appealed to development in order to justify new advances and apparent shifts in doctrine, such as its teaching on religious freedom.

Liturgy and piety

One of the four great constitutions of Vatican II was dedicated to the liturgy. One would like to feel that the document was in the spirit of Newman, with his strong Anglican background. But in Newman's writings one looks in vain for anything resembling the statement of Vatican II that the liturgy is 'the summit toward which the activity of the Church is directed [and] the fountain from which all her power flows.'[20] Much of Newman's piety was aliturgical or paraliturgical, as may be seen from the meditations on the Litany of Loretto, the Stations of the Cross, and the Sacred Heart in his volume of *Meditations and Devotions*. As Ian Ker has noted, Newman's devotion to the Eucharist focuses 'not so much on the Mass as on the Blessed Sacrament.'[21] In his homilies he preached eloquently on the biblical texts assigned for various feasts, but his reflections are rarely inspired by the liturgy. When he speaks of the priestly office of the Church, Newman makes much of popular religiosity, including the cultus of the saints and angels, but he has little to say about ordained priesthood and the ritual action.[22]

As an Englishman Newman felt it difficult to accept some of the extravagances of Italian devotional practices. An instance of Newman's sobriety may be found in his Mariology. He firmly accepted the doctrine of Ephesus that Mary was the Mother of God and the patristic tenet that Mary was the Second Eve. These sources, he believed, gave adequate grounding for the doctrine of Mary's perfect holiness, including her exemption from original sin, which was defined by Pius IX in 1854. But Newman demurred at the exuberance of some authors, who maintained, for instance, that Mary was corporeally present in the Blessed Sacrament or that she possessed priestly powers. Why should we pay dubious honors to Mary, he asked, when there are so many certain ones?[23]

In its Mariology Vatican II follows along the lines indicated by Newman.[24] It quotes many of the same patristic texts that he did in depicting Mary as the Second Eve. Although the Council reaffirmed the essentials of the Catholic doctrinal heritage, it disappointed some Marian enthusiasts by failing to define new privileges of Mary, such as her status as Mediatrix of all Graces or Co-Redemptrix. While Vatican II went beyond Newman in characterizing Mary as a type or figure of the Church, its Mariology, like his, is sober and moderate. It warned against exaggerations and vain credulity.

Ecclesiology

Regarding the nature of the Church, Newman became convinced that the Roman Catholic communion, and it alone, is the 'One Fold of Christ.' He rejected the suggestion that other churches could belong to the body of Christ, although he admitted that individual persons in good faith, but invincibly ignorant of the truth, could belong to the soul of the Church.[25] Vatican II, however, abandoned the distinction between belonging to the body and to the soul of the Church. It taught that non-Catholics and non-Christians might have a salvific relationship to the Church without being fully incorporated into it. It made a distinction, moreover, between the Roman Catholic Church and the 'Church of Christ,' which 'subsisted' in it. This subtle distinction, the precise significance of which is still debated, was not anticipated by Newman.

Newman taught, as the Council was to do, that Christ, who combined in himself the offices of prophet, priest, and king, conferred upon the Church the three tasks of teaching, ruling, and worshiping – that is to say, the prophetic, the regal, and the priestly offices. Vatican II finds these offices concentrated in the hierarchical leadership, which possesses all three in their fullness.[26] The presbyters and the laity are said to participate to a lesser degree in the same three offices. Newman, on the contrary, speaks as though different constituencies in the Church bear each of the offices. The regal office, for him, is concentrated in the pope and the Roman curia; the prophetic is vested in the theologians, and the sacerdotal is exercised by local pastors and laity.[27] By reason of their respective concerns, the holders of the three offices are inevitably brought into tension with one another. In this observation, Newman no doubt expressed an important truth, but not one that I find recognized by Vatican II.

Magisterium and infallibility

The proclamation of binding doctrine was for Newman a task of the regal office. Even in his Anglican days, Newman was convinced that the Church must be able to teach the revelation of Christ with peremptory authority, and in his early works as a Catholic he insisted strongly on the infallibility of the hierarchical leadership.[28] But he did not clearly identify the locus of infallibility. Was it seated in the pope alone, the pope in council, or councils by themselves? After Vatican I he clearly distinguished between two loci of infallibility: the pope in council with the other bishops and the pope acting alone.[29] When speaking of the joint actions of the pope and the episcopate he expressed himself in terms that somewhat resemble Vatican II's teaching on collegial action. But never to my knowledge does Newman describe the body of bishops as a college; he does not see them as having permanent responsibility for the supreme direction of the universal Church. In interpreting Vatican I he follows Bishop Joseph Fessler and other moderates. It would be excessive to hail him as a precursor of Vatican II's teaching on episcopal collegiality.

In his *Letter to the Duke of Norfolk*, Newman at one point indicates that Vatican I's teaching on papal infallibility could be falsely interpreted in a one-sided papalist manner. If this were to happen, he remarked, Providence would undoubtedly supply a later pope who would trim the balance, somewhat as Pope Leo the Great had balanced the teachings of Ephesus by his decisive intervention at the Council of Chalcedon.[30] This remark could be taken as almost a prophecy of Pope John XXIII and the Second Vatican Council, which emphasized the collaborative relationship between the pope and the united episcopate, thus supplying what Vatican I had left unsaid. Newman was careful not to say that Vatican I was itself unbalanced or in need of being trimmed. But he would certainly allow that some interpretations of Vatican I were one-sided and in need of correction.

Roles of theologians and laity

The role of theologians in the Church was a favorite theme of Newman. He often depicted them as a united body, a *schola theologorum*, which could be seen as an authoritative organ for assuring doctrinal orthodoxy. In so doing Newman was looking back nostalgically to the medieval universities, whose faculties of theology exercised a quasi-magisterial role. He lamented the destruction of the Catholic universities and their theology faculties under the modern secular state. Although Newman's views on this point are not without merit, they can hardly be said to have inspired Vatican II. The recent council said very little about theologians. Like Newman, it spoke out in favor of a certain freedom being accorded to theologians, but it does not seem to have envisaged theological faculties as acting corporately or as authoritatively judging the orthodoxy of novel opinions.

In writing about the laity, Newman assumes that their normal vocation is to engage in secular rather than ecclesiastical pursuits. While he wants them to know their creed and their catechism well enough to defend the basic teachings of the Church, he does not encourage them to enter into theological technicalities, any more than he thinks it proper for ecclesiastics to meddle in law, medicine, and finance. He did not want the Catholic university in Ireland to teach dogma *in extenso* to lay students or to treat them as though they were seminarians.[31]

The teaching of Vatican II on the vocation of the laity is generally in line with Newman's views. In its Decree on the Apostolate of the Laity and its Declaration on Christian Education, Vatican II emphasizes the vocation of lay persons to be involved in the world and to bear witness by their way of life rather than by their mastery of theology. But the Pastoral Constitution on the Church in the Modern World expresses the hope that more lay people will pursue theological studies – a hope that Newman shared in some degree. The Council also affirms that the laity should be free to express themselves about matters in which they enjoy competence.[32]

Consensus of the faithful

Newman's famous essay *On Consulting the Faithful in Matters of Doctrine* is often hailed as an anticipation of Vatican II. He aroused some opposition by accusing the bishops of the fourth century of having failed as a body in their duty to defend Nicene orthodoxy. Newman's adversaries did not agree with him that even in the Arian crisis the laity were more orthodox than the hierarchical teachers. He eventually published an abbreviated version of his essay in which the more inflammatory sentences were omitted.[33]

The closest approximation of Newman's thesis on the consensus of the faithful occurs in the Constitution on the Church. In Article 12 it asserts that the faithful as a universal body have received the anointing of the Holy Spirit, and corporately possess a supernatural sense of the faith that cannot be deceived. When the official teachers and the laity universally agree on a matter of faith, their collective judgment is infallible. This statement can be read as echoing Newman's essay. But the idea that the People of God as a whole was infallible in believing had already been a staple of Catholic theology for several centuries and had recently been taken up by Giovanni Perrone and others.[34] Pius IX, as Newman himself observed, had already sought out the opinions of the faithful before the definition of the dogma of the Immaculate Conception. Thus the influence of Newman on Vatican II, even if real, would not seem to have been decisive.

The reception of papal or conciliar teaching by the great body of the faithful had, for Newman, a certain evidential value. As we have seen in Chapter 6, he relied on the reception of the whole body of the faithful to overcome his hesitations about the validity of the dogmatic definition of 1870 on infallibility. In a postscript to his *Letter to the Duke of Norfolk* Newman explains that he did not mean to posit subsequent reception by the Church as a necessary condition of validity. He intended to say only that such reception is an effective way of bringing home to us the authenticity of the teaching.[35]

Vatican II teaches, as did Newman, that popes and councils are able to proclaim the truth infallibly without having to wait on the consensus of the faithful. But it also declares that since the same Holy Spirit is at work in the hierarchical magisterium and in the body of the faithful, such assent will never be lacking.[36] Newman would in principle agree, but so would the vast majority of theologians since the Middle Ages.

In the past thirty years a great deal has been written about the problem of dissent, which occurs when the faithful do not receive, or even reject, the official teaching. Neither Newman nor Vatican II confronts that problem directly. So far as I am aware, Newman never dissented from any official teaching of the Church, nor did he encourage others to do so.

Ecumenical perspectives

In his Anglican days, Newman held that the Catholic Church included a number of communions, of which the Anglican was the one most faithful to Christian antiquity. But when, as a Catholic, he became convinced that the (Roman) Catholic Church was the only true Church, he denied the ecclesial value of other communions. In his controversial writings he tended to be dismissive. He characterized Eastern Orthodoxy as an ossified relic of the past; Anglicanism as a pawn of national governments, and Protestantism as a spurious version of Christianity. Luther, in Newman's view, introduced the fateful principle of private judgment, which eventually came to roost in the skepticism of Immanuel Kant and the rationalism of David Friedrich Strauss.

Vatican II, in contrast to Newman, eschewed polemics. Seeking to build bridges of understanding and agreement, that Council adopted an irenic approach, highlighting beliefs and practices held in common. Thus its posture was quite different from that of Newman the controversialist. Yet the contrast should not be pressed too far, for on occasion Newman could speak appreciatively of the faith and piety of Christians who were not Catholics.

The decisive difference would seem to go back to ecclesiology. For Newman, the Church was fully present or not at all. But for Vatican II, the Church was an organic whole made of up many elements, some of which could be present in the absence of others.[37] Churches and ecclesial communities separated from Rome could possess important elements of the apostolic deposit and thereby mediate grace. They could be, to a greater or lesser degree, in imperfect communion with the Catholic Church.[38] Newman, with his all-or-nothing view of the Church, could not admit that any institution except the (Roman) Catholic Church could be a mediator of grace and salvation, whether to its own members or to non-members. In this respect he differs from most ecumenists of the era since Vatican II.

The religions

Going beyond the standard limits of ecumenism, Vatican II attempted to find common ground among the religions, especially the great monotheistic religions of the West – Judaism and Islam. The Council may be said to have cordially invited these faiths to engage in dialogue with Christianity. Newman lays down certain principles that could provide a basis for a favorable assessment of non-Christian religions. He accepts the universality of divine revelation and the authority of every human conscience. In his sermons he shows deep reverence for the faith of ancient Israel, which he sees as leaning forward to the coming of the divine Messiah. But he shares the polemical attitude of the patristic writers toward Judaism as it has existed since the time of Christ. He considers that because the majority of the Jews failed to believe in Christ, Israel has ceased to be God's chosen people. He is even more unsparing in his denunciation of Islam, which he regards as a violent opponent of the true faith. In these respects his teaching diverges from that of Vatican II.[39]

Religious freedom; Church and State

In its Declaration on Religious Freedom, Vatican II taught that the State should not set itself up as a judge between religions, but should treat all religions as equal before the law. Although the Declaration did not deny the power of the State to establish a particular church, it characterized such establishment as the exception, and insisted that even if one church is officially recognized, freedom of worship should be granted to all.

Newman, in his Anglican period and in his early years as a Catholic, would probably have been uncomfortable with this teaching. As an Anglican he fought against the 'Erastian' subjection of the Church to the State, but he strongly supported the establishment of the Church of England. Repudiating the thesis that 'the civil power has no positive duty, in the normal state of things, to maintain religious truth,'[40] he favored the requirement that acceptance of the Anglican formularies should be made a condition for receiving a degree or teaching appointment at the universities of Oxford and Cambridge. The secular system of education being introduced at the University of London was in his estimation an unwholesome fruit of liberalism.[41] Even as a Catholic Newman continued to maintain that the establishment of Anglicanism was advantageous in restraining the growth of Protestant sects and liberalism. The National Church, as he put it, had thus far functioned as 'a serviceable breakwater against doctrinal errors, more fundamental than its own.'[42]

Maintaining as he did that the State was obliged to uphold religious truth, Newman believed in a certain subordination of the State to the Church. Speaking of the adoption of Christianity as the official religion of the Roman Empire in the fourth century, he wrote: 'If the Church is independent of the State, so far as she is a messenger from God, therefore, should the State, with its high officials and its subject masses, come into her communion, it is plain that they must at once change hostility into submission. There was no middle term.'[43]

As he reflected on the increasing secularization of European culture, Newman became less wedded to the ideal of the 'establishment Church.' He was unenthusiastic about the temporal power of the papacy, which was being contested in Italy. In 1864 he wrote:

> I am not at all sure that it would not be better for the Catholic religion every where, if it had no different status from that which it has in England. There is so much corruption, so much deadness, so much hypocrisy, so much infidelity, when a dogmatic faith is imposed on a nation by law, that I like freedom better. I think Italy will be more religious, that is, there will be more true religion in it, when the Church has to fight for

its supremacy, than when that supremacy depends on the provisions of courts, and police, and territorial claims.[44]

Sentiments such as these are in harmony with the Vatican II's Declaration on Religious Freedom.

Conscience

Newman consistently maintained a very high esteem for personal conscience. The argument from conscience was for him the preeminent proof of the existence of God, arousing an antecedent expectation of a redemptive revelation without which the claims of biblical religion would scarcely be credible.[45] In his *Letter to the Duke of Norfolk* Newman indignantly denied that the Pope had rejected the duty of every human person to follow the biddings of conscience. Following St. Thomas and a multitude of other Catholic theologians, he insisted that conscience is always to be obeyed, whether it be true or erroneous, and even in cases when the individual is culpable for the misguided conscience.

Vatican II, in its Pastoral Constitution on the Church in the Modern World, spoke of conscience in much the same terms as Newman. The Declaration on Religious Freedom likewise asserted that 'in all his activity man is bound to follow his conscience faithfully, in order that he may come to God.'[46] The Declaration used this principle as a basis for the doctrine of religious freedom although, as John Courtney Murray insisted, the Council did not use the ambiguous expression 'freedom of conscience,' nor did it assert that people have a right to do whatever their conscience bids them.[47] On all these points the Council and Newman agree, but it would be difficult to trace Newman's influence on the Council. The teaching of both Newman and Vatican II was based on a longstanding Catholic tradition. Recognizing the accord, Pope John Paul II in his encyclical *Veritatis splendor* quotes Newman's *Letter to the Duke of Norfolk* to confirm the teaching of Vatican II.[48]

Political philosophy

With respect to the political order, Newman was a staunch conservative. A Tory of Tories, he detested liberalism and democratization in politics as in religion. When he was at Algiers on his Mediterranean voyage of 1833, a French ship was also in the port, but he could not even bring himself to look at the detested tricolor on its mast. A little later, on his return trip to England, his coach stopped at Paris for a day, but he kept indoors the whole time because of his hatred for the liberal and anticlerical regime of King Louis Philippe.[49]

In an Appendix to his *Apologia* Newman gives a list of eighteen propositions that he abjured in the 1830s as characteristic of the Liberal party. The list includes the following two:

'16. It is lawful to rise in arms against legitimate princes. Therefore, e.g. the Puritans in the 17th century, and the French in the 18th, were justifiable in their Rebellion and Revolution respectively.

'17. The people are the legitimate source of power. Therefore, e.g. Universal Suffrage is among the natural rights of man.'[50]

Some twenty years later, in a series of letters occasioned by the Crimean War of 1854, Newman found fault with democracy and absolutism alike. He favored a system of government that provided for both protection (which is lacking in democracy) and freedom (which is forfeited in absolutism). By and large – he seems to hold – constitutional government, with its system of checks and balances, works best in times of peace, but in times of war despotism is preferable. The principle of participation, which places no trust in ruling authorities, promotes mediocrity, not excellence.[51]

In contrast to Newman's antidemocratic sentiments, Vatican II, in its Pastoral Constitution on the Church in the Modern World, gave special praise to systems of government that 'afford all their citizens the chance to participate freely and actively in establishing the constitutional bases of a political community, governing the state, determining the scope of various institutions, and choosing leaders.'[52] Without repudiating monarchical government, Vatican II indicated a certain preference for democratic forms.

Newman at his present value

In summary we may say that Newman was on many points in striking accord with Vatican II. He would have welcomed its positions on universal revelation, on the centrality of Christ, on the place of Mary in salvation history, on biblical inerrancy, on the indispensability of tradition, on the authority of bishops, on the consensus of the faithful, and on freedom of conscience. But the Council went considerably beyond Newman in its liturgical directives, its sacramental ecclesiology, its doctrine of episcopal collegiality, its understanding of the threefold office of the bishops, and its ecumenical openness.

Newman's views on the relations between Church and State were not totally in line with Vatican II, but he might have come to agree with that Council's preference for disestablishment. He would probably have been disappointed by certain trends reflected in Vatican II, especially with respect to the historical-critical interpretation of Scripture, the desirability of adaptation to the modern world, and the superiority of democratic or participatory systems of government. Finally, Newman might have wished the Council to say more than it did on certain of his favorite themes, such as the relationship between faith and reason, the role of theologians in the Church, and the homogeneous development of doctrine.

For anyone in search of a theology that is fully Catholic and appropriate to our times and culture, both Newman and Vatican II offer abundant and rich resources. When they agree, Catholics can generally feel confident of their soundness. Where they do not agree, they often supplement each other, offering alternative perspectives that can be helpful for facing the problems of our day. No contemporary theologian can afford to neglect either Newman or the Council.

Newman is an extremely complex figure. His views were in constant evolution as his career passed through successive phases. He frequently framed his arguments polemically, aiming to refute the adversaries with whom he was contending. Even when expounding his personal positions, he could express the objections to them so powerfully that he seemed to be ambivalent about his own stance. Theologians who claim to be his followers tend to quote different passages and thus use Newman against one another. Modernists, liberals, and theological conservatives can all find texts from his writings to support their preferred theses.

After nearly two centuries, the writings of Newman continue to have a very modern ring. His appeal, I suspect, comes not primarily from the acceptability of his conclusions but rather from his highly personal method of arriving at truth. In his letters and diaries, and to a great extent in his works written for publication, we see the mind of the theologian at work, torn by his attraction for each of several incompatible positions. With vast historical learning, he gives telling examples to illustrate the successes and failures of the past. His writings stimulate the reader to replicate the author's own processes of thought. For all these reasons John Henry Newman never ceases to fascinate and to instruct.

Notes

1   JHN to Charles Daniel, 4 January 1867, *The Letters and Diaries of John Henry Newman*, 31 vols. (London: Nelson, 1961–72 Oxford: Clarendon, 1977–), vol. 23, pp. 10–11; hereafter abbreviated *LD*.

2   JHN to Maria Rosina Giberne, 10 February 1869, *LD*, vol. 24, pp. 212–13 at p. 212.

3   Werner Becker, 'Newman's Influence in Germany,' in *The Rediscovery of Newman: An Oxford Symposium*, ed. John Coulson and A. M. Allchin (London: Sheed & Ward, 1967), pp. 174–89, at p. 189. See also in the same volume the essay of B. C. Butler, 'Newman and the Second Vatican Council,' pp. 235–46.

4   In an audience for the Luxembourg Newman Association in 1975 Paul VI declared: 'Many of the problems which he [Newman] treated with wisdom – although he himself was frequently misunderstood and misinterpreted – were the subject of the discussion and study of the Fathers of the Second Vatican Council, as for example the question of ecumenism, the relationship between Christianity and the world, the emphasis on the role of the laity in the Church and the relationship of the Church to non-Christian religions. Not only this Council but also the present time can be considered in a special way as Newman's hour, in which, with confidence in divine providence, he placed his great hopes and expectations,' *L'Osservatore Romano* (Italian language edition), 7–8 April 1975, p. 1.

5   Ian Ker, 'Newman and the Postconciliar Church,' in *Newman Today*, Proceedings of the Wethersfield Institute, 1 (San Francisco: Ignatius, 1989), pp. 121–41.

6   Nicholas Lash, 'Tides and Twilight: Newman Since Vatican II,' in *Newman after a Hundred Years*, ed. Ian Ker and Alan G. Hill (Oxford: Clarendon, 1990), pp. 447–64, at p. 453 and 464.

7   Newman, *Apologia pro Vita Sua* (London: Longmans, Green & Co., 1929), p. 246; hereafter abbreviated *Apol*.

8   Vatican II, Dogmatic Constitution on Divine Revelation, *Dei Verbum*, §2.

9   John Henry Newman, *The Arians of the Fourth Century*, 3rd edn, 1871 (London: Longmans, Green & Co., 1907), p. 87; hereafter abbreviated *Arians*. Newman treats this question in his presentation of the Alexandrian school, with quotations from Clement. Similar ideas reappear in Newman's sermon, 'The Influence of Natural and Revealed Religion Respectively,' Sermon II of his *Fifteen Sermons Preached Before the University of Oxford* (London: SPCK, 1970), pp. 16–36, especially p. 27.

10   See Vatican II, Decree *Ad gentes*, §11, 15; cf. Dogmatic Constitution *Lumen gentium*, §16, Pastoral Constitution *Gaudium et spes*, §22, and Declaration *Nostra aetate*, §2; also John Paul II, Encyclical *Redemptoris missio*, §56.

11   'Letter to the Most Reverend Vincent Nichols,' *Origins* 30 (March 15, 2001), pp. 631–2, quoting the opening sentence of John Paul II, Encyclical *Fides et ratio* (1998).

12   *Dei Verbum*, §11.

13   'It may be almost laid down as an historical fact, that the mystical interpretation and orthodoxy will stand or fall together,' Newman, *An Essay on the Development of Christian Doctrine* (Notre Dame, IN.: University of Notre Dame, 1989), p. 344; hereafter abbreviated *Dev.*

14   *Dei Verbum*, §12.

15   Newman, *The Via Media of the Anglican Church*, 2 vols. (London: Longmans, Green & Co., 1891), vol. 1, p. 273, where he rejects what he regards as the Roman view, that there are some points of faith that rest on tradition without any basis in Scripture; hereafter abbreviated *VM*.

16   Even as an Anglican, Newman rejected the Protestant view that all points of faith can be drawn from Scripture without tradition. See ibid., vol. 1, pp. 273–5.

17   Newman, 'Letter to E. B. Pusey on the Occasion of His *Eirenicon* of 1864,' in Newman, *Certain Difficulties Felt by Anglicans in Catholic Teaching*, 2 vols. (London: Longmans, Green & Co., 1908, 1910), vol. 2, pp. 1–170, at pp. 11–13; hereafter abbreviated *Diff.*

18   Newman, *VM*, vol. 1, p. 288, footnote to Lecture XI.

19   *Dei Verbum*, §9–10.

20   Vatican II, Constitution on the Sacred Liturgy, *Sacrosanctum concilium*, §10.

21   Ker, 'Newman and the Postconciliar Church,' p. 133.

22   Preface to the Third Edition of *Via Media, passim.*

23   Letter to Pusey, *Diff.*, vol. 2, pp. 1–170, at pp. 110–11. Newman is here quoting from the *Diptycha Mariana* of Father Raynaud, SJ

24   See *Lumen gentium*, Chapter 8.

25   Newman, 'Letter to the Duke of Norfolk,' §9, in *Diff.*, vol. 2, p. 335.

26   *Lumen gentium*, §21.

27   Preface to Third Edition of *Via Media*, p. xl.

28   *Dev.*, esp. pp. 78–92.

29   This development in Newman's theology is evident in his 'Letter to the Duke of Norfolk,' esp. §9, 'The Vatican Definition,' in *Diff.*, vol. 2, pp. 171–378, at pp. 320–40.

30   Ibid., p. 307.

31   Newman, *The Idea of a University Defined and Illustrated*, ed. Ian Ker (Oxford: Clarendon, 1976), pp. 376–7 (pagination of uniform edition); *Lectures on the Present Position of Catholics in England* (London: Longmans, Green & Co., 1896), pp. 388–91.

32   Vatican II, *Lumen gentium*, §37; *Gaudium et spes*, §62.

33   *Arians*, n. V, pp. 445–68.

34   See Gustave Thils, *L'Infaillibilité du peuple chrétien 'in credendo': notes de*

théologie posttridentine (Louvain: E. Warny, 1963), where the theme is traced in the work of Melchior Cano, Robert Bellarmine, Gregory of Valencia, Suarez, and many others. Although Thils discusses Newman's contemporaries Franzelin and Kleutgen, he makes no mention of Newman.

35 'Letter to the Duke of Norfolk,' *Diff.*, p. 372.

36 *Lumen gentium*, §25.

37 Ibid., pp. 8 and 15.

38 Vatican II, Decree on Ecumenism *Unitatis redintegratio*, §3–4.

39 For a more detailed discussion of Newman's attitude toward non-Christian religions, see Bertrand de Margerie, *Newman face aux religions de l'humanité* (Paris: Parole et Silence, 2001).

40 *Apol.*, n. A, proposition 12, p. 296.

41 JHN to Archbishop H. E. Manning, 24 November 1873, *LD*, vol. 26, p. 390.

42 *Apol.*, n. E, p. 342.

43 'Letter to the Duke of Norfolk', *Diff.*, p. 201.

44 JHN to William Monsell, 17 June 1863, *LD*, vol. 20, p. 477.

45 Newman, *An Essay in Aid of a Grammar of Assent* (London: Longmans, Green & Co., 1901), pp. 105–21, 415–18.

46 Vatican II, Declaration on Religious Freedom, *Dignitatis humanae*, §3.

47 See footnotes by J. C. Murray to the Declaration on Religious Freedom in *The Documents of Vatican II*, ed. Walter J. Abbott and Joseph Gallagher (New York: America Press, 1966), pp. 679–80, 686.

48 John Paul II, Encyclical *Veritatis splendor*, §34.

49 *Apol.*, p. 33.

50 Ibid., n. A, p. 296.

51 Newman, 'Who's to Blame?' (1855), reprinted in *Discussions and Arguments on Various Subjects* (London: Longmans, Green & Co., 1899), pp. 306–52, especially pp. 306–44.

52 *Gaudium et spes*, §75.

Index

Fleury, Claude   6, 53
Franchi, Alessandro   13
Franzelin, John Baptist   112
freedom, religious   154, 160–2
Froude, Richard Hurrell   3, 4, 5,
   12, 21, 49
Froude, William   12, 49

Galileo   102, 103
Gibbon, Edward   2, 12, 57
Gladstone, William E.   13, 94, 95,
   104
God, proof of   51–3, 59, 138–9,
   162
Gore, Charles   15
grace   19–21, 26, 42–4, 52, 59
   outside Catholic
   Church   118–19, 121, 160
Grammar of Assent, Essay in Aid of
   (Newman)   11–12, 30, 39–42,
   49, 53, 56, 58, 125, 150
Gregory I, Pope   101

Hawkins, Edward   2, 3, 20, 65,
   147
Healy, John   68
heaven   28, 108
hell   28, 30
   eternity of   30, 100
Hilary of Poitiers, St.   106
holiness   2, 19, 25, 30, 90, 155
   of Jesus   59
   see also Church, holiness
Holy Spirit
   conferred in baptism, 21
   directs Church   106, 159
   divinity of   91
   gift   5, 20–3
   indwelling   19, 23, 25, 26, 28
   inspires Scripture   68
Homilies, Edwardian   21, 27
Hügel, Friedrich von   112
Hume, David   1, 34, 35, 39, 44, 49,
   51, 53, 60
Husband, Edward   118

Idea of a University (Newman)   9,
   50, 102–3, 109, 125, 134–47
idea, revelation as   70, 76, 79
Ignatius of Antioch, St.   58
illative sense   40, 43, 150
Incarnation   17, 52, 77, 100, 119,
   125, 140, 152
indulgences   73, 90
   infallibility, consent of faithful
   (reception)   108, 158, 159
   magisterium   89, 90, 101, 112,
   141, 156
   papal   12, 13, 73, 92–6, 128
   necessary for faith   120
Innocent I, Pope   91
intuitionism   37
Islam   118, 160

Jansen, Cornelius   92
Januarius, St.   55
Janus (*see* Döllinger)
Jerome, St.   91
Jesus Christ: center of creation
   (John Paul II)   145, 163
   divine and human   16, 108, 125
   holiness of   59
   image of   58
   sufferings   18
   resurrection   18–19
   see also Christology
Jews   56, 57, 160
John Paul II, Pope   45, 144–6, 153,
   162
John XXIII, Pope   157
Joint Declaration on Justification,
   Lutheran/Catholic   25
judgment
   divine   29, 30
   private   99, 100–1, 105, 120, 159
Julius I, Pope   91
justification   5, 18, 19–28
   see also Christology

Kant, Immanuel   44, 60, 159
Keble, John   3, 5, 21, 37